SOLAR SYSTEM

SOLAR SYSTEM

Bill Yenne

Crescent Books
New York

Page 1: **A photograph of Neptune taken by Voyager 2 during its historic August 1989 encounter. This false color image is among the last full-disk photos that Voyager 2 took before beginning its endless journey into interstellar space.**

Page 2-3: **Saturn and its largest satellites—Dione, Tethys, Mimas, Enceladus, Rhea and Titan.**

This 1991 edition published by Crescent Books, distributed by Outlet Book Company, Inc., a Random House Company, 225 Park Avenue South, New York, New York 10003

Produced by
Brompton Books Corporation
15 Sherwood Place
Greenwich, CT 06830

ISBN 0 517 06528 2

8 7 6 5 4 3 2 1

Printed and bound in Hong Kong

CONTENTS

What is The Solar System? 6

The Sun	12	Jupiter's Moons	44
Mercury	16	Saturn	52
Venus	18	Saturn's Moons	58
Earth	24	Uranus	62
Earth's Moon	28	Uranian Moons	64
Mars	32	Neptune	66
Martian Moons	38	Neptune's Moons	70
The Asteroids	39	Pluto	76
Jupiter	40	Glossary	78

Index 79

Captioned by Bill Yenne and Annie McGarry.
Designed by Bill Yenne.
Photos courtesy of the National Aeronautics & Space Administration with a special thanks to Jurrie van der Woude at the Jet Propulsion Laboratory.

These pages: This color image of the Sun, Earth and Venus was taken by the Voyager 1 spacecraft on 14 February 1990, when it was approximately 32 degrees above the plane of the ecliptic and at a slant-range distance of approximately 4 billion miles (6.4 billion kilometers). It is the first—and may be the only—time that we will ever see our Solar System from such a vantage point.

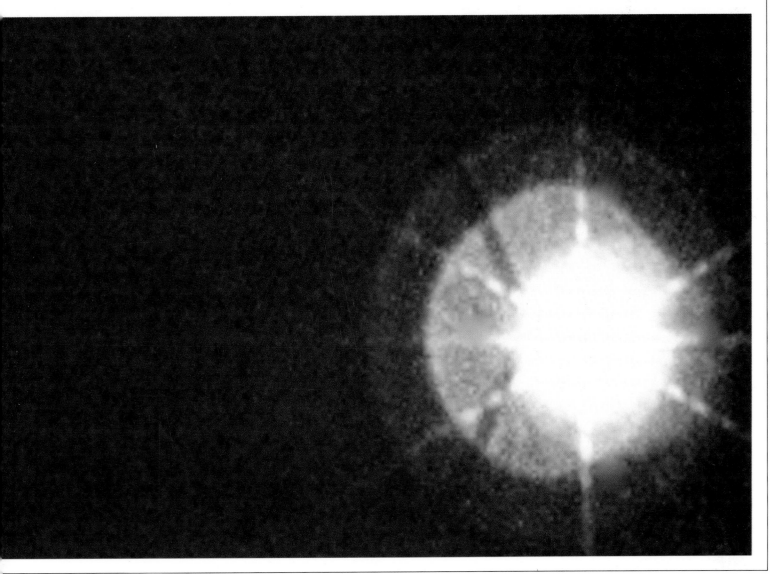

WHAT IS THE SOLAR SYSTEM?

Above: **Meteorites provide enigmatic views of the geology of the Solar System because they are frequently composed of rock types unlike anything that exists on Earth. It is thought that some meteorites may have had their origin in other planets or within the Asteroid Belt.**

Opposite: **This montage of photographs taken by various NASA spacecraft displays the smaller planets and larger moons of the Solar System at the same scale.**

The Solar System can be defined as our Sun and those planets, such as our Earth, which revolve in orbit around it. The Sun itself accounts for 99 percent of the mass of the Solar System, and most of the balance is made up by the nine known planets and their moons (which are in orbit around their planets as those planets are in orbit around the Sun). Other objects within the Solar System include asteroids, or minor planets, which number more than 3000 and exist primarily in a belt between the orbits of Mars and Jupiter. Also present are meteoroids— small fragments of rock which exist throughout the Solar System, but which are too small to be seen until they plunge into the Earth's atmosphere, leaving their disctinctive fiery trails. More spectacular are comets, which are icy objects that appear to take on great fiery tails when their extremely elliptical orbits bring them close to the Sun.

Known as meteoroids when outside a planet's atmosphere, as meteors when falling through the Earth's atmosphere, and as meteorites when they are found intact or when referring to their craters, these relatively small bodies exist throughout the Solar System and frequently impact other bodies in The Solar System.

Despite their small size, meteorites are an extremely important component of the Solar System because their impact craters have contributed extensively to the surface texture of nearly every planet, moon and asteroid.

Meteorites created the features by which we recognize various bodies in the Solar System, and they provide us with the means to determine the sequence of events in a body's history.

With most of the extremely large meteorites expended in the first half billion years, the Solar System's moons and planets have been subjected to a constant bombardment of smaller particles for four billion years. On planets and moons without atmospheres the meteorites simply strike the surface full force. In the case of those with atmospheres, however, all but the very largest burn up in the atmosphere, briefly becoming fiery-tailed meteors or shooting stars—the very bright ones being called fireballs.

The Solar System can be organized into six parts or zones. First, there is the cozy, innermost zone comprised of the terrestrial, or solid surfaced, planets (Mercury, Venus, Earth and Mars), with their total of only three moons, which span the first 150 million miles from the Sun. Next, there is the Asteroid Belt, which spans the 350 million-mile distance from the orbit of Mars to the orbit of Jupiter. Most, but not all, known

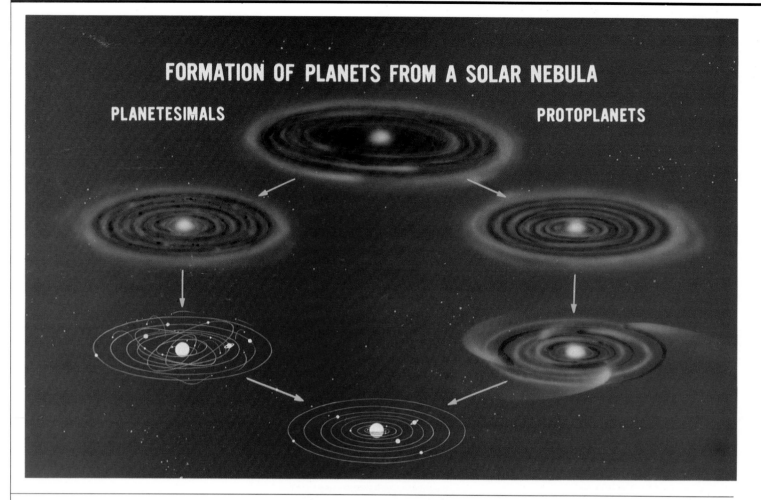

FORMATION OF PLANETS FROM A SOLAR NEBULA

PLANETESIMALS   PROTOPLANETS

THE PLANETS

	Diameter	Average Distance from the Sun	Number of Known Moons	Closest Visit by a Spacecraft from Earth
Mercury	3031 mi (4878 km)	36 million mi (58 million km)	0	Mariner 10 (1974)
Venus	7521 mi (12,104 km)	67 million mi (108 million km)	0	Venera 11-14 Landers (1978-82)
Earth	7926 mi (12,756 km)	93 million mi (150 million km)	1	—
Mars	4212 mi (6794 km)	141 million mi (228 million km)	2	Viking 1, 2 Landers (1976)
Jupiter	88,650 mi (142,984 km)	483 million mi (779 million km)	16	Voyager 1, 2 (1979)
Saturn	74,565 mi (120,000 km)	885 million mi (1.4 billion km)	21 +	Voyager 1, 2 (1980-81)
Uranus	32,116 mi (51,800 km)	1.7 billion mi (2.9 billion km)	15	Voyager 2 (1986)
Neptune	30,775 mi (49,528 km)	2.8 billion mi (4.5 billion km)	8	Voyager 2 (1989)
Pluto	1375 mi (2200 km)	3.6 billion mi (5.9 billion km)	1	None (None planned)

asteroids are to be found within this belt.

Beginning 500 million miles from the Sun, and spanning a distance of 2.3 billion miles, the third and widest zone includes the four largest planets (Jupiter, Saturn, Uranus and Neptune), along with their 50 moons. These planets are identified as 'gas giants' because of their composition and because they are much larger than any other body in any other zone.

The final zone of the *familiar* Solar System contains the planet Pluto and its single moon, which orbit in an elliptical path that ranges between 2.7 and 4.6 billion miles distant from our Sun.

Somewhere in the region of five billion miles from the Sun—nobody really knows—there lies the heliopause, the place where the Sun's influence becomes negligible. Beyond the orbit of Pluto and beyond the heliopause, however, there are two clouds of comets, the inner of which spend part of their orbital lives deep within the inner zones of the Solar System and extend 930 billion miles, while the second of the two clouds of comets extends from 55 to 75 trillion miles.

The Solar System originated 4.6 billion years ago, when protostellar (nebula) material, a hot, swirling cloud of mostly pure hydrogen gas (the simplest of elements) gradually collapsed—succumbing to gravity—and cooled. Gravitational contraction heated this protostar and, in turn, a nuclear fusion reaction was sparked amid the hottest and densest gas that condensed by centrifugal force at the center, and the Sun was born.

The planets were formed from the remaining disc of material still swirling around the Sun, although theories about exactly how this happened disagree. The four largest planets were, and remain, composed largely of hydrogen as well as helium. As such, they and the Sun are relics of the cloud of protostellar nebula material that existed 4.6 billion years ago. The silicate rock, metals, oxygen, nitrogen, carbon and other materials found in the other planets and moons are probably relics of the impurities that existed in the original cloud. Heavy elements are believed to originate in other, more massive stars. They are, in turn, distributed through space when these stars explode as supernovas.

The Solar System displays several fundamental regularities in its structure. This seems to indicate that the mechanisms which formed the Solar System were not random, but rather were the actions of orderly (if not fully understood) physical processes. The planets are not randomly arranged, but rather have regular concentric, near-circular (except for Pluto) orbits. They all revolve in the same direction, and all of the major bodies revolve around the Sun in a relatively flat plane. Using the Earth's orbital plane as the zero degree plane, the orbital planes of all of the other planets tilt no more than 3.39 degrees, except for those of Mercury (7.0 degrees) and Pluto (17.2 degrees).

Each of the two major groups of planets contains *four* major bodies that are as similar to one another as they are dissimilar to the planets in the other group. The terrestrial planets range in diameter between three and eight thousand miles, while the gas giants have a size range almost exactly ten times greater. The terrestrial planets all

Opposite: The hypothetical formation of planets from a solar nebula.

THE MOONS
OF THE INNER SOLAR SYSTEM

	Discovery Date	Diameter	Distance from Planet
Mercury	None		
Venus	None		
Earth	prehistoric	2160 mi	252,698 mi
Luna (the Moon)		(3476 km)	(406,676 km)
Mars			
Phobos	Asaph Hall, 1877	14 mi	5760 mi
		(23 km)	(9270 km)
Deimos	Asaph Hall, 1877	7.5 mi	14,540 mi
		(12 km)	(23,400 km)

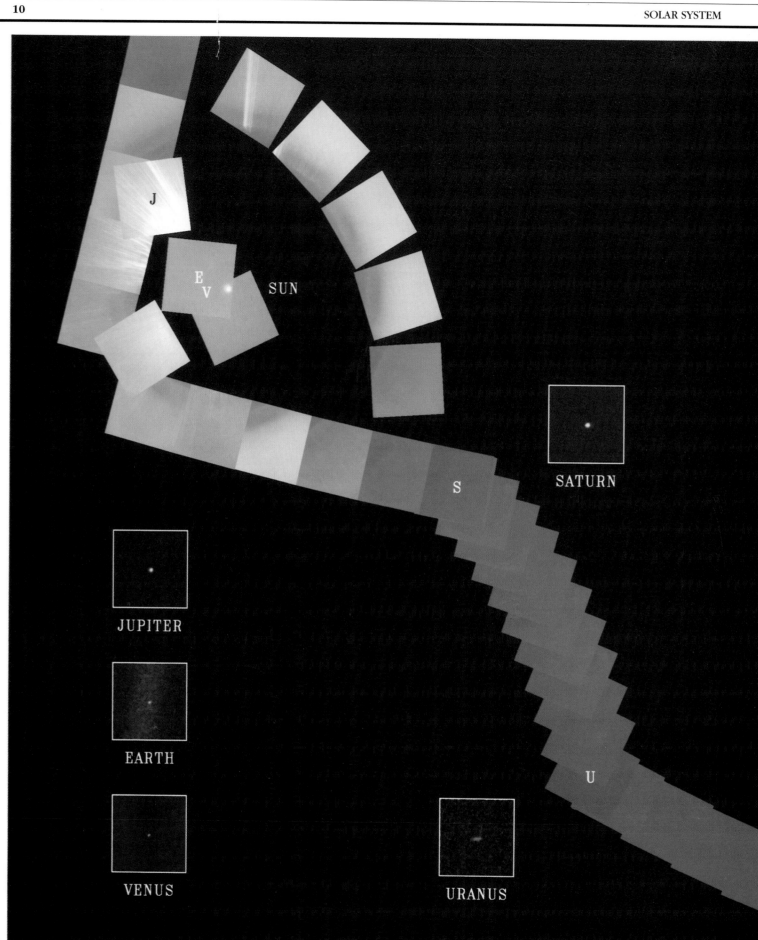

have solid silicate rock crusts with interiors that are (or once were) molten, while the gas giants are balls of hydrogen and helium and bear a closer resemblance to the composition of the Sun than they do to the composition of the terrestrial planets. The four terrestrial planets have just three moons between them, while the four gas giants have at least 50 among *them*.

The compositions of the moons of the outer planets are, however, intriguingly similar to that of the terrestrial planets themselves. Almost all of them are composed of water, ice and silicate rock. Because of their hydrogen/helium composition, the gas giants are known to be closely related to the Sun and so their moon systems could be looked upon *almost* as solar systems within a solar system. Jupiter, for example, is known to have originally been a star whose origin was much like that of the Sun, but which was not massive enough to have undergone self-sustaining fusion reactions.

The bodies in the Solar System can be classified in another important way. Out of the more than 3000 planets, moons and asteroids in the Solar System, only *eight* are known to have atmospheres consisting of more than barely detectable traces of gases near their surfaces. These include the four gas giants, of course, which could be described as being almost *all* atmosphere. The others are the terrestrial planets Venus, Earth and Mars, as well as Saturn's moon Titan. Of these four, Venus and Titan have atmospheres that are so thick that their solid surfaces are completely obscured by clouds.

The objects in the Solar System can also be classified by their surface type. Again, of course, the gas giants with their gaseous 'surfaces' are in a class by themselves. Another class would be those with silicate rock surfaces that have been marked primarily by meteorite impact craters. This class would include Mercury, the Earth's Moon, the Martian moons and all the asteroids. A third class, the so-called 'dirty snowballs,' are composed mostly of silicate rock and water ice marked by meteorite impact craters and some inherent geologic activity. This class would include nearly all the moons of the outer Solar System's four gas giants.

The Solar System is an amazing place, full of intriguing similarities and inexplicable peculiarities. It is amazing both in its orderliness and its diversity. It interests us and confuses us, for as much as we are able to learn, our new knowledge serves only to inspire new questions.

NEPTUNE

N

Above: Comets are essentially 'snowballs' of carbon dioxide, methane or water ice that have extremely elliptical orbits and which exhibit spectacular tails when heated by the Sun. This 'snowball,' usually containing a solid core, is the permanent part of the comet and is known as its nucleus. The cometary nucleus is usually quite small. Halley's Comet, for example, has an irregular nucleus that is only about nine miles long and five miles wide. The nucleus, in turn, is surrounded by a hydrogen cloud.

As the nucleus nears the orbit of Mars on its journey inward from the distant reaches of the Solar System, interaction with the solar warmth causes it to develop a fuzzy halo, or coma. (The word coma, as used here, is the Latin word for 'hair,' rather than the Greek word for 'deep sleep.') As the nucleus and coma reach the orbit of the Earth, a tail begins to develop as the Solar Wind blows material away from the nucleus. Upon the formation of the tail, the coma is known as the comet's head. Tails may be composed of particulate impurities released from the nucleus, in which case they will appear curved. Tails may also be composed of ionized gases, in which case they will be straight.

Opposite: The first ever 'group portrait' of the Solar System as seen from the outside. On 14 February 1990, the cameras of Voyager 1 took a series of pictures of the sun and the planets from a distance of approximately 4 billion miles (6.4 billion kilometers). This mosaic consists of a total of 60 frames.

THE SUN

The engraving *above* depicts solar flares as seen during an eclipse.

Opposite: **A huge solar eruption can be seen in this spectroheliogram obtained during the Skylab 3 mission in 1974. This photograph reveals for the first time that helium erupting from the Sun can stay together to altitudes of up to 500,0000 miles (800,000 kilometers).**

Giving life to both living organisms and human legends, the Sun is the central body of the Solar System, although until just a few hundred years ago, it was thought to be in orbit around the Earth! Technically, the Sun is an average-sized star of the yellow dwarf variety that formed roughly 4.6 billion years ago at the center of that enormous swirling gas cloud which became the Solar System. The concentration of pressure at the center of this swirling cloud of (mostly) hydrogen triggered a nuclear fusion reaction. In this fusion reaction, typical of all stars, four nuclei of hydrogen atoms (the simplest of the elements) fused to form a single helium atom (the second simplest element, having two protons) nuclei. The resulting reaction released a tremendous amount of energy.

Though it is not considered to be a particularly large star, the Sun is by far the largest body within the Solar System, containing 99 percent of all its matter, and thereby providing the gravitational force that literally *defines* the Solar System and controls the orbital paths of the other bodies within it. The Sun is also the source of most of the heat in the Solar System, and thus it provides the warmth that makes life possible on at least one of the bodies in the Solar System. The temperature at the core of the Sun is estimated at roughly 70 million degrees Fahrenheit, the surface temperature averaging 11,000 degrees Fahrenheit. The energy radiated from the Sun is called solar radiation, which (as measured in wavelengths from the longest to the shortest) can be simplified as including: (a) radio waves, (b) microwaves, (c) infrared radiation (perceived on Earth as heat), (d) the visible light spectrum, (e) ultraviolet radiation, (f) x-rays and (g) gamma rays. So powerful is solar radiation that its ultraviolet wavelengths can tan (or burn) human skin on Earth and direct light from the visible spectrum can do permanent damage to the human eye.

Like the other major bodies in the Solar System, the Sun rotates on its axis. However, its equatorial region rotates once every 27.375 days, while its polar regions have a slower rotational period of 34 days.

The Sun, being a gaseous sphere, has no solid surface, nor could any molecular solid exist at such incredible temperatures. The Sun does, however, have a nearly opaque surface—a sea of gaseous firestorms known as the photosphere.

The firestorms that comprise the photosphere are roughly 600 miles in diameter and appear as granules in the vastness of the scale of the Sun. Their apparent opacity is due to the presence of negative hydrogen ions. During the approximate eight-minute

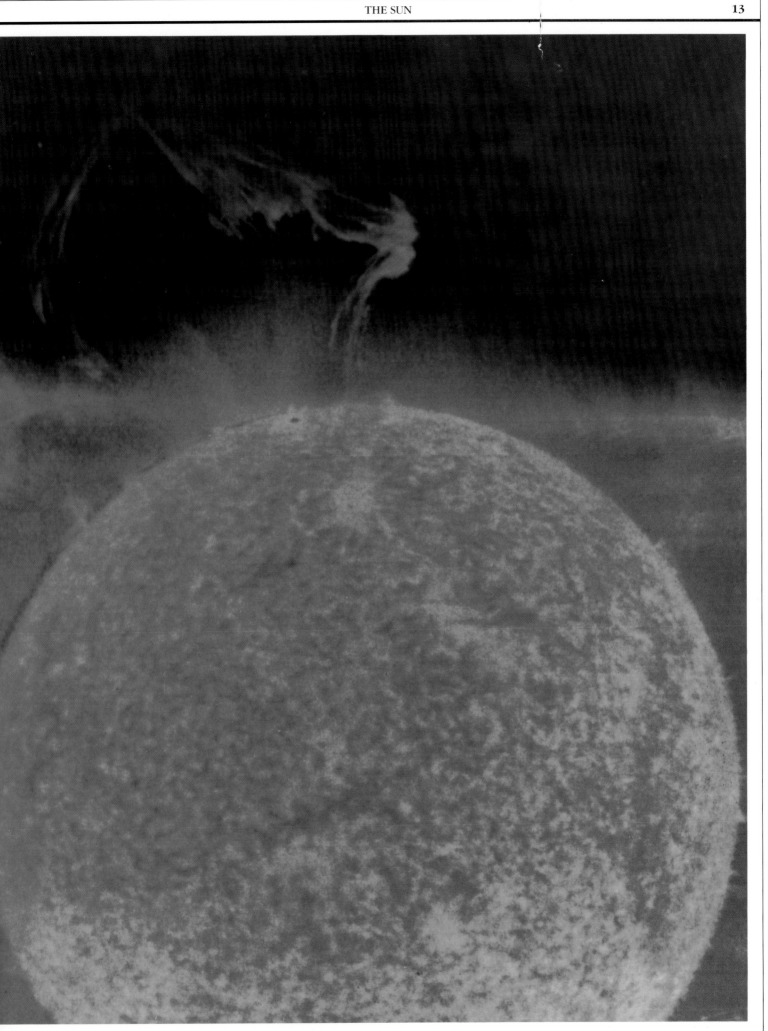

Above: **A drawing of a sunspot observed on 5 March 1873. Sunspots are dark regions on the surface of the photosphere which are cooler than the surrounding areas. Man has been observing this phenomenon for many years.**

lifespan of the granule, hot gas rises out of the center, pushing cooler gases aside and into the narrow darker and cooler spaces between the granules. Amid the typical granules, there are 'supergranules,' with diameters up to 18,000 miles and lifespans of up to 24 hours.

Other 'surface features' on the photosphere are solar flares and sunspots. Solar flares are violent surface eruptions that explode from the photosphere with the energy of 10 million hydrogen bombs, sending forth a stream of solar radiation that can disrupt radio signals on the Earth.

Solar flares were first observed in 1859 by the English astronomer Richard Carrington. They have also been observed to a greater or lesser degree on other stars. The frequency of solar flares can range from several in a single Earth day during periods when the Sun is active, to fewer than one per Earth week during the periods that astronomers describe as 'quiet.' The energy for individual flares may take several hours or even days to build up, but the actual flare, when the energy is released, happens in a matter of minutes. The resulting shockwaves travel outward across the photosphere and up into the chromosphere and corona for hundreds of thousands of miles at speeds on the order of three million mph.

It is not known what triggers solar flares, but magnetic energy almost certainly plays a major role. The study of solar flares is important because of the effect on Earth of the radiation and particles released during solar flares, not to mention the potential negative effect on spacecraft and astronauts beyond the Earth's atmosphere. The charged particles released in the flares are attracted by the Earth's magnetic field and spiral in at the north and south magnetic poles, causing the Aurora Borealis in Earth's atmosphere.

Sunspots are dark regions on the surface of the photosphere which are cooler than the surrounding areas. Like the solar flares, sunspots occur with less frequency during the Sun's quiet periods. During such periods there may be *no* observable sunspots, while during active periods there may be more than a hundred on the photosphere at one time.

Sunspots were first observed by the Chinese 2000 years ago, and in the seventeenth century, the great Italian astronomer Galileo Galilei (1564-1642) conducted a systematic study of them. His observations of the motion of sunspots across the solar surface led to his discovery of the rotation of the Sun. The frequency of

sunspot activity has been recorded as occurring in an 11 year cycle that seems to have an effect on the weather on Earth. The period from 1645 to 1715 was, for example, an era of a very quiet Sun and for *seven years* during this time *no* sunspots were observed. These years also corresponded with the height of the cold spell in the Earth's northern hemisphere that is referred to as the 'little ice age.'

Sunspots vary in size and shape and may be as large as 40,000 miles across. They are composed of a 'penumbra' with a darker 'umbra' in the center (which constitutes about a quarter of the sunspot's area). Sunspots increase to their full size in about a week to 10 days, but in turn take nearly two weeks to decay. Sunspots usually occur in groups, and a large group may have a life span of several weeks.

It is not known what causes sunspots, but the standard theory has it that a powerful magnetic field temporarily restricts the flow of the hottest gasses to that particular part of the photosphere; sunspots seem to appear at places where magnetic field lines have become twisted and rise above the photosphere.

Above the photosphere there is a thinner, more visually transparent layer known as the chromosphere (literally 'color sphere'). This layer is roughly 6000 miles thick. The most common feature within the chromosphere are the spicules, long thin fingers of luminous gas which appear like a vast field of blades of fiery grass growing up into the chromosphere from the photosphere. They are observed to rise to the upper reaches of the chromosphere (about 6000 miles above the photosphere), and then drop back in about 10 minutes.

Beyond the chromosphere is the corona, a vast field of hydrogen particles that extends for millions of miles into space. The corona is so sparse that it is not visible against the glare of the Sun—except during a total solar eclipse when the Moon passes between the Earth and the Sun, blotting out the photosphere. During periods of quiet Sun, the corona is more or less confined to the solar equatorial regions, with corona holes being present in the polar regions. During periods of more activity, the corona is evenly distributed around the Sun, including the polar regions, but appears most prominent near the regions of the most sunspot activity.

The corona is mysteriously hotter than the photosphere, despite the second law of thermodynamics which holds that heat cannot be conducted from the cooler to the warmer. The mystery involves the process by which the corona is heated. The dynamics of solar magnetic fields and acoustic energy are suggested as possible answers. Despite its high temperature, the corona's very low density means that it radiates relatively little energy.

Blowing outward from the Sun and its corona is a constant stream of hot, ionized, subatomic particulate plasma known as the solar wind. A constant phenomenon, the solar wind gusts from 450,000 mph to two million mph, and blows into the distant reaches of the Solar System. By definition, the place where the solar wind no longer blows is the heliopause.

The solar wind spirals out from the Sun, rotating with the Sun until it reaches a distance of approximately 100 million miles. From that point it travels outward with less interference from the Sun's magnetic field.

Below: **The relative intensity of solar regions is color coded in this ultraviolet spectroheliograph. White is the greatest intensity, followed by yellow, red and blue. The spectroheliograph was transmitted to the Goddard Space Flight Center from the latest of the Orbiting Solar Observatory series spacecraft, OSO-7.**

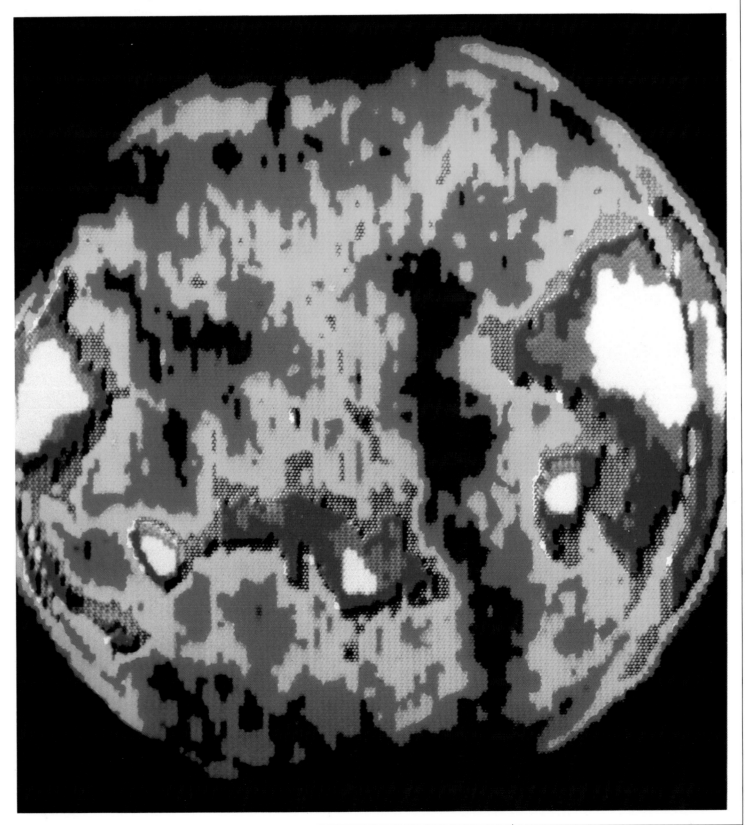

MERCURY

Above: **Mariner 10 was 49,000 miles (77,800 kilometers) distant when this photograph of Mercury was taken. This view of Mercury's northern limb shows a prominent east-facing scarp extending from the limb (near the middle of the photo) southward for hundreds of kilometers.**

The linear dimension along the bottom of the photo is about 365 miles (580 kilometers). The 'tear' in the limb near the top of the picture was caused by a loss of data. Mariner 10 encountered Mercury on 29 March 1974, passing the planet on the dark side 431 miles (690 kilometers) from the surface.

Because of its proximity to the Sun, Mercury is always observed within 27 degrees of the Sun in the east before sunrise or in the west after sunset. The closest planet to the Sun and the second smallest of the nine planets, it has been observed from Earth since prehistoric times. However, because of its size it is fainter than Venus, Mars, Jupiter and Saturn—the other planets visible to the naked eye.

Mercury has a sidereal period of just three months, the shortest of any planet. Because of this, it has the appearance from Earth of moving faster than the others, a characteristic which led the Greeks to name it Hermes, after the messenger of the gods. The Romans, in turn, called the planet Mercury after their own deities' wing-footed messenger.

Johann Hieronymus Schroeter (1745-1816) became the first astronomer to record his observations of Mercury's surface detail, but his drawings, like those of Giovanni Schiaparelli (1835-1910) more than a century later, were ill-defined and turned out to be inaccurate. The great American astronomer Percival Lowell (1855-1916) reported that he had observed streaks on Mercury's surface similar to those that he and Schiaparelli had both observed on Mars. Schiaparelli had called these Martian features canali (channels) and Lowell decided they were *canals*, built by intelligent life. Both astronomers agreed, however, that the streaks on Mercury's surface were of natural origin. The major milestone in the observation of Mercury came in March 1974 when the American spacecraft Mariner 10 began a series of three flybys at a distance of about 12,000 miles, in which it was able to photo-graph, in great detail, objects as small as 325 feet across.

The Mariner 10 photos revealed a planet whose surface features could easily be mistaken for those on the Earth's Moon. Like the Lunar surface, that of Mercury is pocked by thousands of craters. With the exception of the relatively smooth Caloris Basin, Mercury's surface is characterized almost exclusively by craters, overlapping craters and craters within craters. The Lunar surface, by contrast, has more larger open areas known as maria, or seas. The Caloris Basin, which is itself pocked by hundreds of relatively smaller craters, is the only major open plain comparable to the Moon's maria. Unlike the Lunar seas, which are ancient lava flows, it is believed that the Caloris Basin was created by a massive, ancient impact, as is indicated by the presence of mountains and ridges around its periphery, possibly caused by seismic waves. Other ridges and escarpments are to be seen on the surface, and are possibly due to the expansion and contraction of Mercury's core as it cooled and shrank. Some of the cliffs produced by this effect rise as much as 6300 feet above the adjacent valley floors. There is some evidence of ancient volcanic activity on Mercury, but less than that of the Moon.

Because of Mercury's overall density, its core is thought to be largely (70 percent) composed of iron, with the surface crust being silica rock, like that of the Earth or Lunar surfaces. Due perhaps to its slow rotation, Mercury has a relatively weak magnetic field, despite its being composed mostly of iron.

Unlike the other three inner terrestrial planets, Mercury has virtually no atmosphere. Faint traces of gaseous helium form 98 percent of the 'atmosphere,' with the remainder being composed mostly of hydrogen, with minute traces of argon and neon also being present. The helium was probably captured from the Sun, because any gasses emanating from the interior of the planet would have long ago dissipated into space.

Mercury's surface temperatures vary widely. The midday temperature on the side facing the Sun can be as hot as 610 degrees Fahrenheit, while at night temperatures can plummet to -346 degrees Fahrenheit because there is no atmosphere to hold the heat.

Below: **A mosaic of over 200 High-Resolution Mariner 10 photographs shows Mercury's southern hemisphere as it would appear from 31,000 miles (50,000 kilometers) away. The bright rays which dominate the surface are from fresh impact craters. The large craters are approximately 106 miles (170 kilometers) across.**

VENUS

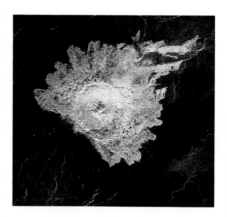

Above: **The impact crater Aurelia. In 1990, Magellan radar-mapping confirmed earlier hypotheses (based on earlier radar mappings of the enigmatic cloud-covered planet) that Venus is a rugged, cratered terrain.** *Opposite:* **The Pioneer Venus Orbiter took this photograph, showing the 'ashen light' once believed to be Venusian city lights, but now known to be electrical storms.**

As viewed from Earth, Venus is the brightest celestial object in the sky except for the Sun and Moon. Like the Moon, Venus can be seen to go through a series of phases as it orbits the Sun and is viewed from Earth. The Greek poet Homer even went so far as to call it the most beautiful star in the sky, while the Romans named it Venus after their goddess of beauty. The second planet from the Sun, Venus is a near twin of the Earth in terms of size, with a diameter 95 percent that of our own planet. Like Mercury, and unlike every other planet in the Solar System, Venus has no moon.

Transits—in which the planet passes directly between the Earth and the Sun—are characterized by an effect similar to an eclipse, although Venus appears as a mere tiny black dot creeping across the face of the Sun. Transits are rare, occurring in pairs eight years apart—and then not at all, for well over a century. The last pair of transits, for example, occurred in 1874-1882, and the next will occur in 2004-2012.

Any attempt to see the surface features of Venus were frustrated by the fact that the entire surface is covered by a thick cloud layer, a fact not known to early astronomers. Giovanni Cassini (1625-1712) produced the first 'map' in 1667, but as cloud patterns changed he could no longer find the features he had drawn. Johann Hieronymus Schroeter (1745-1816) was also fooled and reported having seen mountains on the surface. Schroeter, however, *was* the first to observe a very real phenomena, that of the 'ashen light' seen in the Venusian atmosphere on the dark side of the planet. This faint light was at one time thought to be the city lights of Venusian civilization, but is now attributed to lightning which occurs during the planet's frequent electrical storms.

By the early twentieth century, it had been determined that the Venusian surface was obscured by clouds, and various theories evolved regarding the actual nature of the surface beneath those clouds. The nineteenth-century idea that the planet was covered by lush jungles was dismissed in favor of the two schools of thought that suggested either a vast desert or a vast ocean of water.

It had been established that the surface would be extremely hot because carbon dioxide in the thick atmosphere would prevent solar heat from escaping the surface, thus producing what is referred to as a 'greenhouse effect.'

The first successful expedition to the vicinity of Venus came in December 1962 when the American unmanned spacecraft Mariner 2 traveled to within 21,600 miles

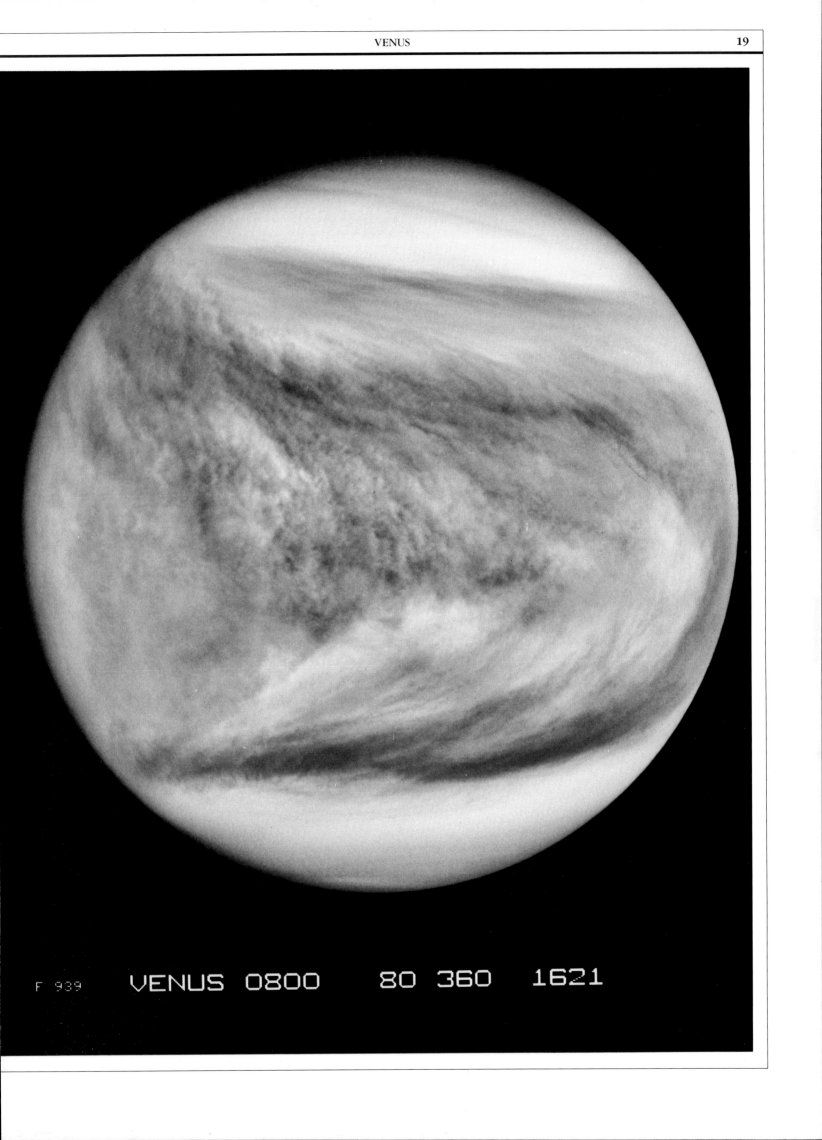

F 939   VENUS 0800   80 360 1621

Below: **False color perspective of Danu Montes (upper center). Ten percent of Venus' terrain is very mountainous.**

of the planet. The flight of Mariner 2 was a major milestone in unlocking the secrets of the mysterious planet. Among its achievements were confirmation that Venus has no detectable magnetic field, confirmation of the planet's exact rotational period—245 Earth days—and confirmation that it rotates from east to west, rather than the opposite as previously supposed.

Mariner 2 also provided a more accurate reading of the planet's surface temperature, which at 900 degrees Fahrenheit is too hot for the existence of an ocean, because water could exist there only as steam. Water vapor is in fact present in the atmosphere, and some astronomers have theorized that at an early stage in the evolution of Venus, oceans *may have* in fact existed on the surface.

In 1978 the United States undertook the Pioneer Venus project as a follow-on to several earlier Mariner probes. The project consisted of an Orbiter spacecraft and a Multiprobe spacecraft. The former under-

took the detailed radar mapping of the Venusian surface that made possible the maps on these pages, and which gave us much of the information we now have about the planet's terrain. The Multiprobe was actually five probes designed to return data about the Venusian atmosphere as they plunged toward the surface. One of the Pioneer Venus Multiprobes continued to return data from the surface for just over an hour after impact.

The Soviet Union, meanwhile, prepared a series of spacecraft to conduct soft landings on the Venusian surface, which returned the only photographs ever taken of the Venusian surface. The Soviet Venera 9 and Venera 10 spacecraft each returned a single black and white image in 1975, and the Venera 13 and Venera 14 spacecraft returned color photos in March 1982.

While the Soviet Venera spacecraft provided the first photographs of specific points on the Venusian surface, the American Pioneer Venus Orbiter provided our

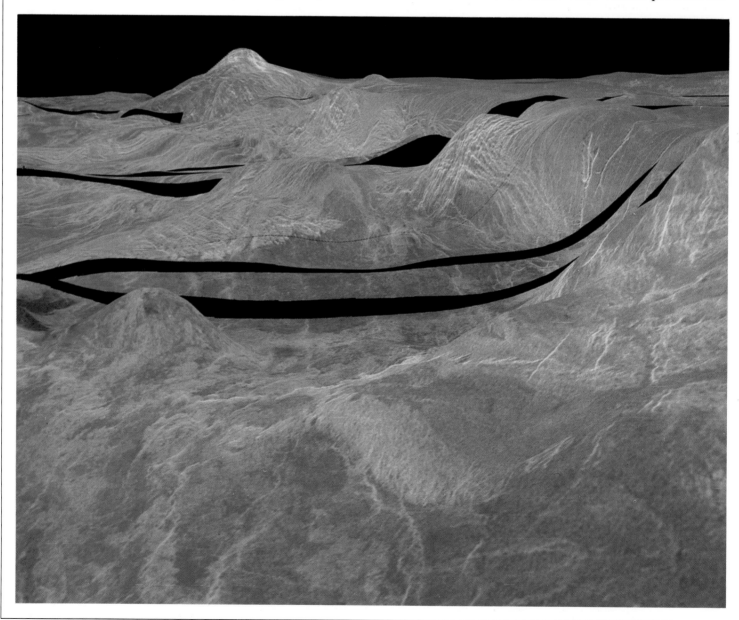

first clear look at the overall global surface features of Venus.

Using a radar altimeter, Pioneer Venus was able to obtain the data necessary to produce a topographical map of 90 percent of the planet's surface, from 73 degrees north latitude to 63 degrees south latitude.

On 4 May 1989, the United States used the Space Shuttle Orbiter Atlantis to launch the four-ton Magellan radar-mapping spacecraft on a mission to Venus. Arriving at the cloud-shrouded planet on 17 August 1990, Magellan initially conducted 1852 mapping swaths around the planet, a process which continued for 243 Earth days, or one Venusian day. The resolution of the data returned by Magellan was vastly superior to that achieved by Pioneer Venus a decade earlier. Indeed, the quality of the imagery was so good that the data it transmitted looked like actual photography of a cloudless planet!

Satellite data from Pioneer Venus in 1978-1979 was thought to show that the surface was generally smoother than those of the other three terrestrial planets, but in 1990, Magellan, which was capable of 'seeing' in more detail, revealed a more rugged terrain. However, Magellan confirmed Pioneer's findings that Venus has much less variation in altitude than is seen on Earth. For instance, 60 percent of the Venusian surface is within 1600 feet of the planet's mean radius of 3752 miles. It has been suggested that this is due to the deeper lowlands having been filled with sand and other wind-blown material. Because there are no seas on Venus, the mean radius is used as a reference point in the same way that sea level is used on Earth.

Most of the surface of Venus is characterized as rolling uplands, rising to an altitude of roughly 3000 feet, while 20 percent of the surface is identified as lowlands and 10 percent as mountainous. The two largest upland regions, or continental masses, are Aphrodite Terra (roughly the size of Africa), near the equator in the Southern hemisphere, and Ishtar Terra (roughly the size of Australia), in the northern hemisphere near the North Pole. These two features constitute the Venusian 'continents' and are named respectively for the ancient Greek and ancient Babylonian goddesses of love.

The highest points on the mapped surface of Venus are in the Maxwell Mountains (Maxwell Montes) in Ishtar Terra. High enough to have been identified by Earth-based radar prior to the Pioneer Venus project, the Maxwell Mountains, which may

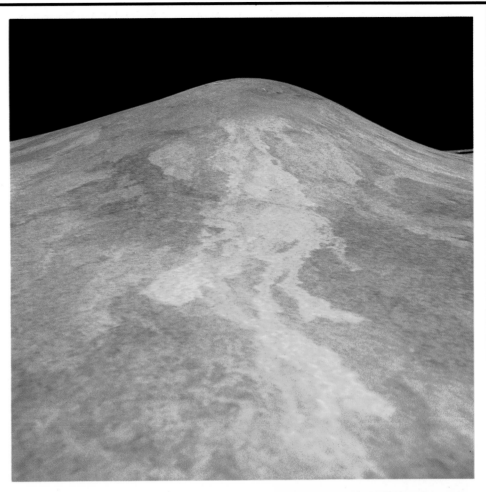

actually be a single mountain, rise to more than 35,000 feet above mean radius, or roughly 20 percent higher than Mount Everest rises above Earth's *sea level*. If viewed from the surface they would be an impressive sight, rising nearly 27,000 feet above Lakshmi Planvin, the surrounding plateau which is roughly the same elevation as the Tibetan plateau on Earth.

Data obtained from Pioneer Venus indicates that the Maxwell Mountains may be the rim of an ancient volcano whose caldera had a diameter of roughly 60 miles. The lava flows, however, have long since been worn away by wind erosion, and the slopes of the Maxwell Mountains are strewn with rocks and debris.

Another important upland region is Beta Regio with its great shield volcanos, Rhea Mons and Theia Mons, which are larger than the great shield volcanos of Hawaii on Earth. The mountainous Beta Regio is still in the process of formation and probably contains active volcanos. As such, it is the newest major surface feature on Venus.

The lowest point on the Venusian surface is actually a canyon, Diana Chasma, located within central Aphrodite Terra. At just 9500 feet below mean radius, Diana Chasma is much shallower than the corresponding lowest point on Earth, the Marianas Trench. The largest and lowest

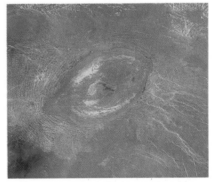

Top: **False color perspective of the volcano Sif Mons. Some Venusian volcanos are believed to be still active.** *Bottom:* **A false color image of the Sacajawea Patera Volcano.**

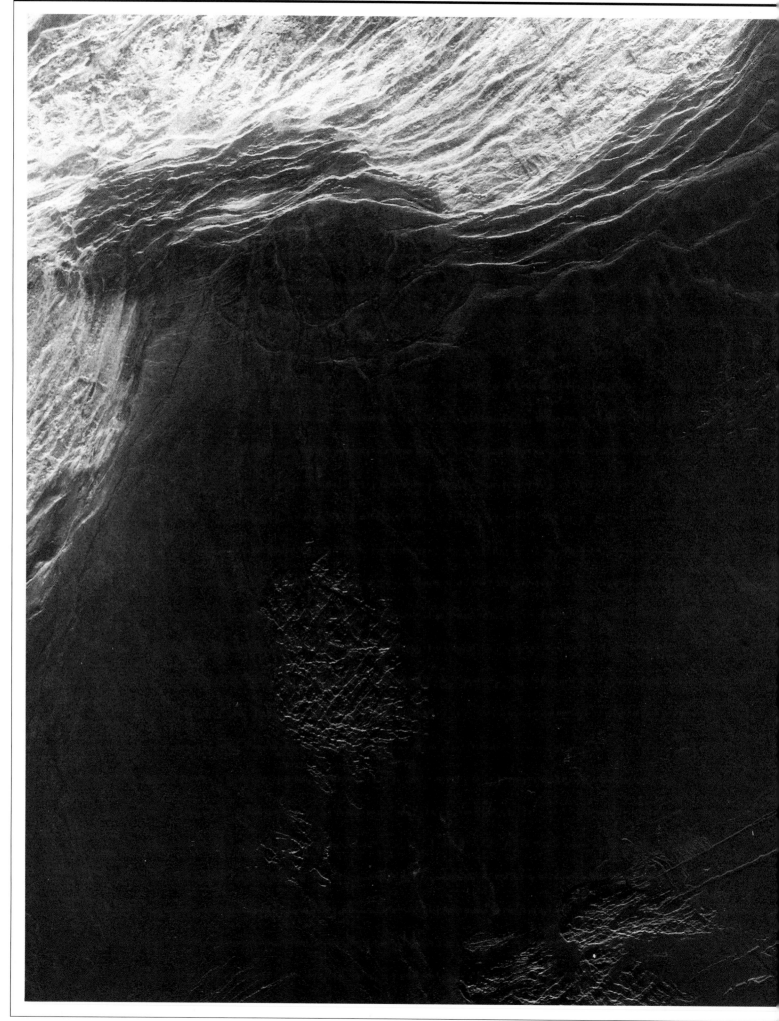

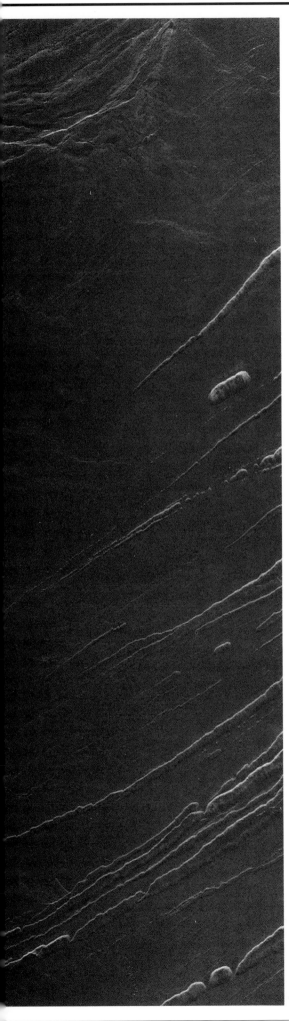

lowland region on Venus is the Atalanta Plain (Atalanta Planitia) located northeast of Aphrodite Terra and due east of Ishtar Terra. It is roughly the same size as the Earth's North Atlantic Ocean, although it is shallower by comparison.

The atmosphere of Venus has long been known to consist primarily of carbon dioxide, and the instruments of Pioneer Venus and Venera have pinpointed the proportion of carbon dioxide at 96 percent. Nitrogen constitutes more than three percent of the Venusian atmosphere, and there are also traces of neon and several isotopes of argon.

There is some water vapor present in the Venusian cloud cover, where it has a density of 200 ppm—ten times the density of water vapor in the clear air near the surface. In the clouds the water vapor combines chemically with traces of sulphur dioxide to produce droplets of sulfuric acid, which give the Venusian cloud cover its distinctive yellowish color.

The Venusian cloud cover is complete and unbroken. The cloud layer is roughly 15 miles thick, with its base about 30 miles above the surface of the planet, relatively higher than the thinner cloud cover on Earth. The air at the surface is probably quite clear and the air relatively still. The clouds, however, are pushed by winds with speeds up to 200 mph and circulate around the entire planet once every four Earth days, in contrast to the rotation period of Venusian 'day,' or 243 Earth days. Electric storms are common within the clouds and lightning has been detected by both American and Soviet spacecraft.

The most notable visible feature in the Venusian atmosphere, and one that misled so many would-be mapmakers in earlier days, is the Y Feature, whose tail sometimes stretches around the planet. The feature is actually the prevailing winds in the northern and southern hemispheres as they diverge at the equator. This pattern is constantly changing, and sometimes it is seen as a reversed C. It always, however, retains an approximate north-south symmetry.

On the surface of Venus, atmospheric pressure is roughly 100 times that of the Earth. A yellowish glow like that of a smoggy sunset on Earth is all pervasive. The daytime surface temperature of 900 degrees Fahrenheit is a global constant because the carbon dioxide and sulfuric acid atmosphere and cloud cover function as an insulating blanket, trapping the heat and producing convection currents that redistribute it across the entire surface area.

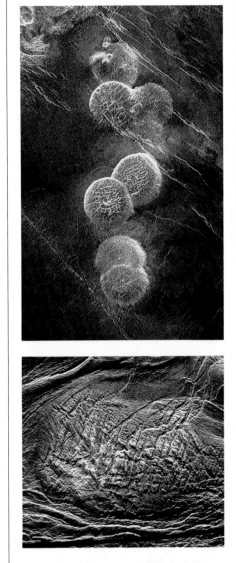

Left: This stunning Magellan full resolution radar image shows the eastern edge of Lakshmi Planum and the western edge of Maxwell Mountain. The plains of Lakshmi are radar-dark, smooth, homogenous lava flows. Located near the center of the image is a feature previously mapped as a tessera made up of intersecting graben. The distinct outline of this feature indicates that it has been partially covered by lava.

Along the left hand side is Maxwell Montes, the highest mountain on the planet, and part of a series of mountain belts surrounding Lakshmi Planum. The western edge of Maxwell shown in this image rises sharply, three miles (five kilometers) above the adjacent plains in Lakshmi Planum.

Top: Magellan at Venus. 'Pancake' Volcanic Domes. This phenomenon is still somewhat of a mystery.

Above: Another shot from Magellan, of the fractured dome in Freyja Montes. The 'turtle-back' appearance is due to two sets of intersecting fractures.

THE EARTH

Above: **The mountains of North America, formed when the continental plates collided, have been further shaped by eons of wind and water erosion.**

Opposite: **A view approaching Cuba and Florida from the south. Light cloud cover partially obscures the Atlantic Ocean and the Gulf of Mexico. At any given moment half the Earth's surface is covered with clouds.**

The Earth is the only planet in the Solar System where life is known to have evolved, and because it is our home planet, we know more about its physical characteristics than we do of the other planets. However, if we were viewing it from Mars or Venus, we would soon calculate that it is the third planet from the Sun and largest of the four terrestrial planets.

When The Solar System was formed 4.6 billion years ago, the Earth was probably solid throughout, but 500 million years later, radioactive decay heated the planet, and gradually metallic material melted and separated from nonmetallic silicate material and sank toward its center, while the silicate floated up. This molten metallic material, consisting mostly of iron with some nickel, survives today as the Earth's core, which is approximately 4200 miles in diameter. At temperatures of approximately 11,000 degrees Fahrenheit, the core is mostly molten, although a solid inner core, perhaps 200 miles in diameter, is thought to exist at the center of the Earth. The constant motion of the molten core gives the Earth its magnetic field.

Outside the core is the layer known as the mantle. Composed largely of both solid and molten silicate rock, it is roughly 1800 miles thick. Covering the mantle is a thin crust, which ranges from 25 to barely five miles thick. Occasionally, hot molten rock from the mantle forces its way through the crust in the form of lava during volcanic eruptions. So thin is the crust that it exists as a group of separate continental plates that literally float on the semi-liquid mantle, a phenomenon called continental drift. The edges of the continental plates are the faults and rift zones where volcanic activity and earthquakes are most common.

The Earth's oceans provide a convenient means of reckoning what is known on other solid-surface planets as the mean surface altitude (mean radius), which is referred to on Earth simply as sea level. The highest region on the continental mass of the Earth is the Tibetan plateau and the accompanying Himalaya Mountains, which are located within the Eurasian Continent. The 47 tallest mountain peaks on Earth are located in this region. The tallest of these, Mount Everest, stands 5.5 miles above sea level. By comparison, the Maxwell Mountains on Venus rise to 6.6 miles above mean radius, while Mount Olympus on Mars towers 15.5 miles above mean radius. Meanwhile, the lowest point on the Earth's surface is the Challenger Deep in the Marianas Trench of the Pacific Ocean, which is

At top: The rocky Pacific coast of America, the jagged seam between two plates. Around every major ocean, especially the Pacific, the oceanic crust is either pushed or drawn back down toward the mantle. The frictional convergence of continental and oceanic crust can cause such geological pranks as earthquakes and volcanos.

Center and above: These satellite false color images of two Total Ozone Mapping Spectrometer (TOMS) compare the ozone holes in 1988 and 1990. The ozone hole is seen as the pink and darker pink colors.

seven miles below sea level. Again, by comparison, the floor of the Diana Chasma on Venus is 1.8 miles below mean radius and the Hellas Basin is 1.9 miles below the mean radius of Mars.

Because of the effects of wind and water erosion, the meteor impact craters, common to such other inner terrestrial bodies as Mercury, Mars and the Earth's own Moon, are rare on the Earth. The effect of water alternately freezing and thawing also has a tendency to break up the rocks of the Earth's mountains. Consequently, the newly formed ranges on the Earth, such as the Rocky Mountains (which are between 70 and 300 million years old), tend to be higher than the more ancient ranges—such as the Appalachians, which are at least 400 million years old. The Earth's mountains were originally formed by the pressure of the continental plates moving against one another, and through volcanic action. Most of the ranges were formed by the former process, although the latter takes a relatively shorter time and is a good deal more spectacular. The sea mounts (mountains whose base is on the ocean floor, but whose top may be above sea level) of the Hawaiian Island chain are a good example of the latter, and the Island of Hawaii, with its three active volcanos (Mauna Kea, Mauna Loa and Kilauea) is a good example of a sea mount that is still in the process of growing.

After the Jovian moon Io, the Earth is the second most volcanically active body in the Solar System, with Venus and Neptune's moon, Triton, being the only other bodies where volcanic activity is probably occurring at this time. The most volcanically active area on Earth is the Pacific Basin, with volcanos active not only in Hawaii but also in an arc around the north Pacific rim, that stretches from Indonesia to Japan and Alaska and down the west coast of North America to the Cascades range, where the 1980 eruptions of Mount St Helens in Washington were very spectacular. Other volcanically active regions include the Italian peninsula and the North Atlantic (particularly Iceland).

Above the surface of the Earth is its atmosphere, which is comprised of several layers of gases roughly 120 miles thick and weighing 5700 trillion tons. Composed primarily of nitrogen (78 percent) and oxygen (21 percent), the Earth's atmosphere is divided into five layers. The troposphere is the thickest and closest layer, covering the Earth to a depth of seven miles. Next are the stratosphere or ozonosphere (7 to 30 miles), the mesosphere

(30 to 50 miles) and the ionosphere (50 to 150 miles). Roughly 80 percent of the Earth's atmospheric molecules and most atmospheric pressure are concentrated in the troposphere. While the composition of the Earth's atmosphere is the same at all altitudes, clouds of water vapor are concentrated only in the troposphere. The atmosphere becomes much thinner above the mesosphere, so that 120 miles altitude is generally recognized as the edge of outer space. However, some remnants of Earthly atmosphere exist above 120 miles, so that the upper ionosphere and the region beyond is subdivided into the thermosphere (60 to 400 miles) and the exosphere (beyond 400 miles). The Earth's atmosphere serves to shield the planet from much of the Sun's radiation. The visible spectrum penetrates all the atmospheric layers, but infrared and radio waves are partially blocked by the stratosphere. Ultraviolet radiation is almost entirely blocked by a layer of ozone in the stratosphere, and x-rays do not penetrate the mesosphere. The Earth's atmosphere also acts as a modulator of temperatures. Had the Earth been slightly warmer, it would have suffered the same sort of greenhouse effect that befell Venus and would today also have a carbon dioxide atmosphere.

The Earth's 23.4 degree inclination of its axis produces the seasonal effect, wherein the northern and southern hemispheres are alternately closest to the Sun. Only twice each Earth year, on the vernal and autumnal equinoxes, will the Sun shine directly on the Earth's equator. In the northern hemisphere, for example, the inclination toward the Sun increases from the vernal equinox (21 March) until the summer solstice (21 June). At the summer solstice, the northern hemisphere is oriented so that it receives the most sunlight of the year, while the southern hemisphere receives the least. From the summer solstice until the autumnal equinox (23 September), the amount of sunlight gradually decreases in the northern hemisphere and increases in the southern, as the Sun is perceived to cross the equator. On the autumnal equinox the Sun 'crosses' the equator, and the trend continues until the winter solstice (21 December) when the most sunlight reaches the southern hemisphere and the least sunlight reaches the northern hemisphere. After the winter solstice, the Sun's warmth once again moves north toward the equator and the northern hemisphere, and the seasonal cycle goes around again and again. The Sun is directly overhead only at the equinoxes. This regular annual pattern determines the climate of all the regions of the Earth.

Changes in the axial inclination, which varies by as much as 2.5 degrees in 100,000 years, can produce such dramatic changes in climate as the Ice Age, which covered 25 percent of the Earth's land area with ice until 15,000 years ago.

Throughout the Earth's annual seasonal cycle, its equator receives more sunlight than any other part of the planet, while the poles receive the least. For this reason, the Earth's poles have permanent ice caps which recede slightly with their respective warmer seasons, but which are always present. In the south polar region there is the ice covered continent Antarctica, while in the north polar region there is the ice covered Arctic Ocean. The Antarctic ice cap contains about 6.3 million cubic miles of frozen water, while the Arctic ice cap and associated North American and Eurasian glaciers (including Greenland) contain 680,000 cubic miles of water.

The inclination of the Earth to its axis and the resulting seasonal effect produce annual changes in temperature and pressure. These, in turn, control the Earth's global weather pattern and the movement of the clouds. The mountains on the Earth's continents can, in turn, affect weather by triggering precipitation on their windward side.

The complex interrelationship of axial inclination, chemical composition and geographical composition that is unique to the Earth probably played an important role in the development of the phenomenon of life. Earth is the only planet in the Solar System, and indeed in the Universe, where life is known to exist. While it is possible that some form of life will be found to exist or to have once existed on another body in our Solar System, it is hard to imagine a world with anything to match the abundance of plant and animal life forms that have developed on the Earth over the past two billion years.

Above: **The 'backbone of North America,' the Rocky Mountains edge the continental plate. Oceanic material, sedimentary strata and volcanic rock accumulate, are buried, lifted, deformed and eroded to form such fold mountain ranges.**
Below: **The Guadalupe Mountains of New Mexico clearly show evidence of very ancient stratification followed by erosion.**

EARTH'S MOON

Above: **An Apollo 10 westward view across Landing Site 3 in the Central Bay. The prominent crater Bruce near the bottom of this photo is 3.7 miles (roughly 6 kilometers) wide.** *Opposite:* **This outstanding view of a near full moon was photographed from the Apollo 13 spacecraft during its journey homeward. Though the explosion of an oxygen tank forced the cancellation of the scheduled lunar landing, Apollo 13 made a pass around the Moon. Some conspicuous lunar features include the Sea of Crisis, the Sea of Fertility, the Sea of Tranquility, the Sea of Nectar and the Sea of Vapors.**

Although it is the second brightest object in the sky, all of the light from the Earth's moon—like that of the planets—is reflected from the Sun. Some tiny portion of the Moon's light could be called Earthshine, as noticed during a crescent phase when the 'dark' part of the Moon is slightly illuminated. It is light from the Sun reflected by the Earth to the Moon, which, in turn, reflects it back to Earth. The Earth's single satellite is mythologically associated with Luna (or Diana), the Roman goddess of the hunt, who was also their goddess of the Moon. The sixth largest moon in the Solar System, the Moon is closer in size to its mother planet than any other except Pluto's moon Charon. For this reason the Earth and the Moon (like Pluto and Charon as well) are occasionally described as being a double planet. While the larger planets have on the order of a thousand times the mass of their moons, the Earth has 81 times the mass of the Moon and four times the diameter.

The Moon is the only other object in the Solar System to have been visited by human beings from the planet Earth. In 1968 the United States began the Apollo project, a series of space flights during which the Moon became the first body in the Solar System beyond Earth to be explored firsthand by human beings. The Moon was surveyed by human beings from Lunar orbit for the first time by means of two circumlunar manned flights in December 1968 and May 1969, which began the operational phase of the Apollo program. In July 1969 the Apollo 11 spacecraft became the first vehicle to land human beings on the Moon. The initial landing was followed by six others between November 1969 and December 1972. (A seventh mission was aborted because of hardware failure in April 1970.)

During the Apollo program, 12 American astronauts conducted detailed surveys on the Lunar surface and seismic studies of the Lunar interior. The Apollo program completed detailed mapping of the Moon and provided a wealth of information about its composition and its geologic history.

As perceived from Earth, the Moon appears to go through a series of phases depending upon its reflection of light from the Sun. These phases, which constitute the Lunar 'day,' go through a complete cycle every 29 days, 12 hours and 44 minutes. The cycle is also known as the synodic, or Lunar month, as seen on Earth.

When the Moon is fully illuminated it is said to be 'full.' As the visible face of the Moon rotates away from the Sun it is said to be 'waning.' When exactly half the *face* of

At top: **The Lunar Module 'Intrepid'
with astronauts Charles Gordon, Jr
and Alan Bean, separated from the
Command Module 'Yankee Clipper'
with Richard Gordon aboard. The
module comes in for a landing in the
Ocean of Storms. The large crater on
the right is named for astronomer
William Herschel.**
Above: **In lunar orbit, the Apollo II
approaches landing. This view of the
southwestern Sea of Tranquility
looks generally west. The large crater
at lower right is Maskelyne.**

the Moon is illuminated, it is called a 'quarter Moon.' As it becomes less visible it is
said to become a 'crescent Moon,' and
when it becomes dark and the cycle is
resumed, the Moon is said to be a 'new
Moon.' From 'new,' the Moon waxes
through the crescent phase to the quarter
phase, and once again to full. The Sun
always illuminates one-half the Moon.
Depending upon the relative angle
between the Earth and Moon, we see por-
tions of the sunlit side. At 'full Moon' we see
the entire sunlit side, and at 'new Moon'
none of the the sunlit side is facing the
Earth.

The Moon's period of rotation is 27 days,
seven hours and 43 minutes—nearly the
same as the period of its revolution around
the Earth, so the same side always faces the
Earth. Because of the Moon's slight wob-
bling, we are able to see slightly more than
half of its surface from the Earth. The
Moon's mysterious far side had been a mystery to mankind for centuries, and it was
not until the Soviet Luna 3 spacecraft
returned photographic images of the 'dark
side of the Moon' in October 1959 that
actual detailed information of the Moon's
'other half' was revealed to mankind.
Though the 41 percent of the Lunar surface
that is never visible from the Earth is frequently referred to as the 'dark side,' it
actually receives as much light from the
Sun as the near side.

The Moon's surface is characterized by
rugged mountain ranges and by thousands
of meteorite impact craters. In this sense it
is very much like the planet Mercury.
Unlike Mercury, however, the Moon has
large open areas that are called seas (or in
Latin, *maria*) because to the eye they
appear darker than the surrounding terrain, and were once thought by Galileo to
resemble seas. Almost entirely concentrated on the side facing the Earth, the
maria cover 15 percent of the Lunar surface, and were probably once 'seas' of molten rock that flowed out of the Moon's
interior. The gravitational effect of the
Earth probably has a great deal to do with
the fact that such features are concentrated
on the Earthward side.

Unlike the Earth, the Moon has neither
magnetic poles nor a significant magnetic
field, although rocks in the Lunar crust are
weakly magnetized. Probably due to its low
mass and density, the Moon never developed
an atmosphere, although trace amounts of
hydrogen and helium, as well as hints of
argon and neon were detected as escaping
from the Lunar surface in 1972 by the crew
of the American Apollo 17 spacecraft.

The Apollo program studies revealed
that the Lunar interior was quite active,
with moonquakes being more common on
the Moon than earthquakes are on the
Earth, although they have not been
recorded in excess of two on the Richter
scale.

The Moon formed about the same time
as the Earth—4.6 billion years ago—and is
composed of the same basic materials, but
their early relationship is unclear. One line
of thought theorizes that the Moon was
formed out of the Earth, either in a single
piece that broke loose (perhaps from the
Pacific Basin) or in the form of debris that
was knocked loose in a collision with an
asteroid, and which eventually congealed
into the Lunar mass. Another theory holds
that the Moon was a separate planet 'captured' by the Earth's gravitational field. A
third notion has it that the Earth and Moon
were formed in the same way and in the
same place and time. Because the Earth was
81 times larger, the Moon became enslaved
to its gravity.

Once in place, the Moon's geology
evolved much like that of the Earth. Originally molten, the crust gradually cooled,
leaving a molten core like that of the Earth.
In the meantime, it was being bombarded
by debris from the formation of the Solar
System. In addition to smaller craters, huge
basins were hammered into the surfaces of
both bodies. Some of the first basins to be
formed in the Moon were Mare Fecunditatius and Mare Tranquilium; they probably formed 4.4 billion years ago. The last
basins to be formed were the Mare
Imbrium and Mare Orientale. Dating from
3.85 billion years ago, Mare Imbrium is the
largest of the Lunar seas, and its origin
concludes the Pre-Imbrian period of Lunar
geologic evolution.

When the Imbrian Period began 3.85
billion years ago, the Lunar surface was
probably pocked entirely and uniformly
with impact craters. The semicircular
mountain ranges found around the periphery of the maria are the only remnants of
the enormous impacts that created them.
During this period, however, intense interior heating resulted in vast flows of darker
basalt from deep within the Moon. Part of
the heating came from meteor impacts, and
part from radioactive decay. These flows
filled the huge basins, and the Lunar seas
briefly were seas—of lava!

When the Moon cooled, and the lava
flows ended 33 billion years ago, small
scale volcanic activity continued for
approximately 1.3 billion years through
what is called the Ratosthenian Period.

During this period, interplanetary debris crashed into the Moon, creating newer, smaller impact craters on the Lunar seas themselves. One of the major craters now visible on the surface, Copernicus, was probably formed one billion years ago, marking the climax of the third period of Lunar geology. Since the formation of Copernicus there has been very little geologic activity on the Moon. This fourth period, the present Copernican Period, has also been marked by very little in the way of impact crater formation, although the crater Tycho is thought to have been formed as recently as one million years ago, and the formation of the great crater Giordano Bruno is believed to have been witnessed from Earth in 1178 AD. In July 1972, a 2200-pound meteorite was recorded as having struck the Moon. Throughout the billion years of the Copernican Period the Moon's surface has remained relatively unchanged because there is no air, no wind and no water to cause erosion of the type that has greatly altered the surfaces of such bodies as the Earth and Mars.

Left: The view from the Apollo 14 Saturn 5 space vehicle. Carrying Astronauts Alan Shepard, Stuart Roosa, and Edgar Mitchell, the nation's sixth manned voyage to the moon lifted off from Kennedy Space Center. Roosa piloted the command module while Shepard and Mitchell descended in a Lunar Module. They remained on the surface 33 hours and spent eight to 10 hours outside of their spacecraft on 5 and 6 February 1971.
Below: Lunar Module pilot James B Irwin gives a military salute while standing beside the deployed United States flag during Apollo 15 extravehicular activity. The Lunar Module 'Falcon' is in the center. On the right is one of three Lunar Roving Vehicles. This photograph was taken by David R Scott, Apollo 15 commander.

MARS

Above: **This is an alternate color version of a Viking 1 picture of Mars. During processing, 40% gray was added. The cable in the foreground, which is actually bright orange, provides a clue to Mars' true colors.**
Opposite: **This scene, an oblique view along the Tharsis Ridge, the major volcanic province of Mars, was taken 13 July 1980 by the Viking 1 Orbiter. The three Tharsis volcanoes, Arsia Mons, Pavonis Mons and Ascraeus Mons (from bottom) rise an average of 10.8 miles (17 kilometers) above the top of the 6.2 mile high (10 kilometers) Tharsis Ridge. Altitudes are figured relative to the lowest point on Mars, because there is no sea level.**

Venus may be the Earth's near twin in terms of size, but Mars has more specific characteristics in common with the Earth than does any other planet. The Martian year lasts 23 Earth months, but the Martian day is only 41 minutes longer than the Earth day, and its inclination of 24 degrees to its rotational axis is very close to the Earth's 23.4 degrees. As a result, Mars has four seasons that parallel those that we experience on Earth. The Martian summer is relatively warmer than its winter, which is characterized in the temperate zones by occasional light snow or frost. Mars is the only planet in the Solar System besides the Earth that has polar ice caps, and these can be seen to expand and recede seasonally like those on Earth. The south polar cap is composed of water ice and carbon dioxide ice (dry ice). The north polar cap is composed only of water ice with merely a residual carbon dioxide snow cover that evaporates in summer. Known as 'The Red Planet' because of its distinctive iron oxide coloration, Mars reminded early observers of a distant bloody battlefield, and the Chaldeans called it Nergal, the furious one. The Greeks and the Romans named it Aries and Mars after their gods of war, and the latter name is still in use. Because of its perceived similarity to Earth, Mars has interested and intrigued Earthbound observers for centuries, and that is certainly still the case in the twentieth century.

Mars is a good deal smaller and less dense than Earth. Because of this, Mars has less gravity and a much thinner atmosphere than Earth. It is also colder than the Earth, with temperatures in the polar regions rarely rising above the −200 degrees Fahrenheit level, although the midsummer temperature near the Martian equator can reach a comfortable 80 degrees Fahrenheit at midday, closer to a consistant 'Earthly' temperature than can be found anywhere else in the Solar System.

The characteristic rust-red Martian surface is indicative of the high concentration of iron oxide in the soil and rocks. The surface of Mars is covered by the types of volcanic and impact craters that are found on Mercury or on the Earth's moon, but there are also vast, lightly-cratered plains, particularly in the northern hemisphere. While there are no currently active volcanos on Mars, those dormant volcanos which do exist are the tallest volcanos yet discovered in the Solar System.

The dormant shield-type volcano, Olympus Mons (Mount Olympus), is the tallest mountain on Mars, soaring 15.5

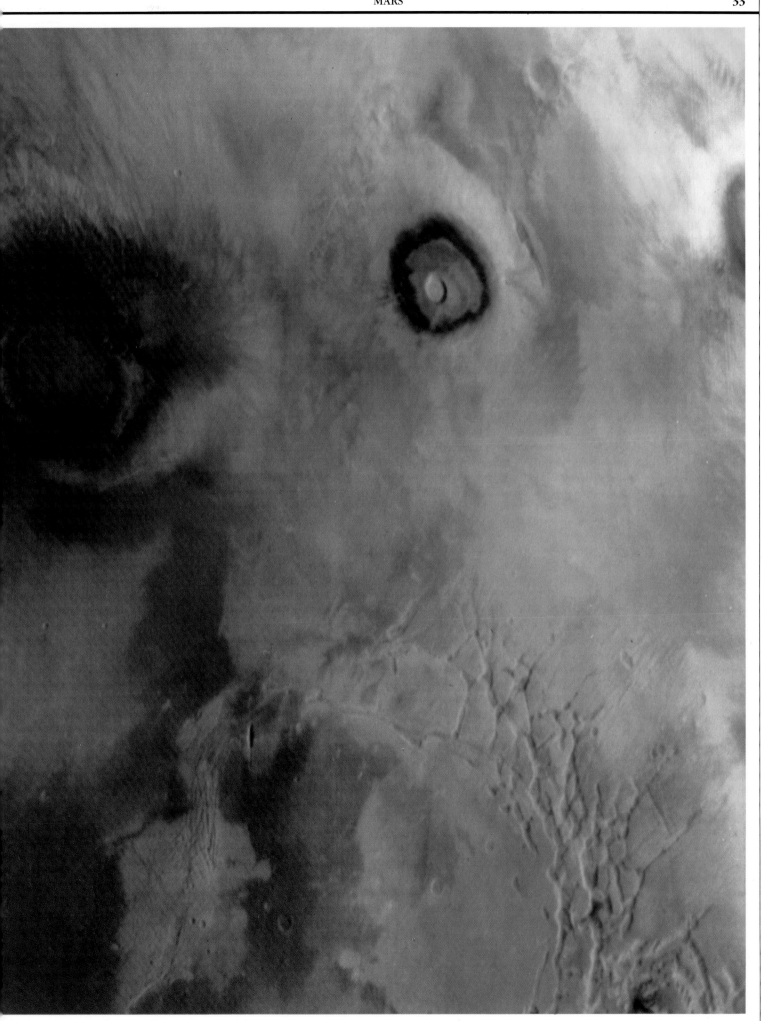

At top, and above: **WR Heigh created these images of Martian flora and fauna in 1907 and 1909. By the mid-19th century, it was widely believed that Mars supported life in some form. Today, the question of whether there is or ever has been life on Mars remains unanswered.**

miles above the mean radius, or standard elevation, of the Martian surface. Mount Olympus stands 10 miles higher than the Earth's Mount Everest and encompasses more than 50 times the volume of Hawaii's Mauna Loa, the largest shield volcano on Earth. Southeast of Mount Olympus, across the plain of the Martian Tharsis Region, stands a neat row of three other large and important shield volcanic mountains—Arsia, Pavonis and Ascraeus. Ancient lava flows from the Martian volcanos helped to create Mars' vast open plains.

Another feature common to other bodies in the inner Solar System are fault rifts and seismic fracture zones. One such large fracture is Valles Marineris (Mariner Valley), a huge canyon stretching east by southeast from the Tharsis Region across the Martian equator. More than 3000 miles in length, Valles Marineris is the largest single surface feature on the planet. More than four times deeper than the Grand Canyon on Earth, it is a network of roughly parallel rift canyons with an overall width of up to 400 miles and a main canyon 125 miles wide at its widest.

There is no liquid water visible at any place on the surface of the red planet, nor is Mars' atmospheric pressure high enough to permit it to exist, yet the riverbeds bear silent witness to the fact that a great deal of water may have once flowed there. The Martian surface is marked by vast networks of dry riverbeds, huge channels cut by former streams of running water. These features defy explanation on a planet whose water is frozen in polar ice caps or trapped deep below the surface in subterranean permafrost.

Beneath the Martian surface is a rigid crust 31 miles thick which probably contains water ice permafrost. The Martian mantle, composed of basalt rock, is roughly 125 miles thick. Beneath the mantle is a partially-molten transition zone leading to a formerly molten core that is between 800 and 1300 miles in diameter.

Like that of Venus, the Martian atmosphere is almost entirely composed of carbon dioxide, with traces of nitrogen, argon and oxygen also present. The atmosphere is divided into three layers, which are (from the densest and closest): the troposphere, which rises to an altitude of 22 miles; the stratosphere (22 to 80 miles), and thermosphere (80 to 140 miles). The exosphere accounts for the residual Martian atmospheric gases that exist above an altitude of 140 miles altitude. Unlike the Earth's atmosphere, that of Mars generally circulates laterally with little interaction

between the weather patterns of the northern and southern hemispheres, the Martian atmosphere has distinct north-south weather patterns that cross the equator.

Mars has much less cloud cover than the Earth's roughly 50 percent coverage, but the cloud types are similar. These include cirrus and gravity wave clouds, as well as cyclonic storms that on Earth would be referred to as hurricanes or typhoons. Low lying areas, such as deep valleys or canyons, develop ground fog as a result of frost being vaporized by the early morning Sun, a phenomenon not uncommon on the Earth.

While most of the Martian cloud cover is composed of water vapor (like the clouds of the Earth's atmosphere), carbon dioxide clouds exist at high altitudes and in the polar regions during the winter. Such clouds may result in precipitation in the form of dry ice snowstorms that play a role in replenishing the polar ice caps. The ice caps are also replenished by carbon dioxide condensation. While the carbon dioxide that is present in the ice caps as dry ice vaporizes and circulates within the Martian atmosphere, polar temperatures are such that most of the water ice present in the Martian ice caps remains frozen continuously, even in summer.

In 1659 the Dutch astronomer Christiaan Huygens (1629-1695), who was the first to identify a Martian surface feature (Syrtis Major), also calculated the Martian day to be almost the same as the Earth's, which it is. Seven years later the Italian astronomer Giovanni Domenico Cassini (1625-1712) discovered the Martian ice caps. By 1783 William Herschel (1738-1822) had correctly calculated the exact length of the Martian day and the exact inclination of Mars to its axis.

By the middle of the nineteenth century the picture painted of Mars was that of a hospitable place that 'certainly' supported life in some form, probably similar to that of Earth. After all, their days were the same length and their seasons were parallel to ours. The darker areas on Mars were thought to represent 'vegetation,' and some observers recorded that this 'vegetation' waxed and waned with the Martian seasons.

In 1877 the Italian astronomer Giovanni Schiaparelli (1835-1910) made a startling discovery. There were channels, or canali, on the surface of Mars! Translated into English as 'canals,' the features were quickly ascribed to artificial origin. It was thought that intelligent creatures had constructed an intricate system of irrigation canals on Mars to bring water from the polar ice caps to the warmer equatorial region.

In 1894 the American astronomer Percival Lowell (1855-1916) opened his observatory at Flagstaff, Arizona primarily for the purpose of studying Mars. Lowell carefully observed and mapped the Martian surface and became a leading exponent of the idea that the canals were constructed by living creatures to irrigate their crops.

In the 1930s Eugenios Antoniadi, a Greek-born astronomer working in France, produced a map of Mars which was quite accurate for its day, but one which rejected the earlier notion of artificially constructed canals. By the late twentieth century the canal theory had been thoroughly discredited as having been an optical illusion, but the idea of Martian vegetation survived until spacecraft visited the red planet.

The first spacecraft to pass near Mars was the American Mariner 4 in 1965, and it was followed by Mariner 6 and Mariner 7, four years later. The data returned by these flybys seemed to confirm the notion that Mars was a dull and lifeless place, roughly cratered and more like Mercury than the Earth.

In 1971, however, the Mariner 9 spacecraft was placed into orbit around Mars. For the first time the full range of the planet's wonders, such as the great shield volcanos and the vast networks of river beds, was revealed. Mariner 9 remained in service until October 1972, by which time the entire Martian surface had been mapped.

In August and September 1975 the United States launched the two identical Viking spacecraft toward Mars. Each Viking consisted of an orbiting module and a landing module designed to make a soft landing on the Martian surface. The Viking project was an outstanding success. The Viking 1 Lander alighted in the Chryse Planitia on 20 July 1977 and continued to transmit data until November 1982. The Viking 1 Orbiter conducted a close-up reconnaissance of the Martian moon Phobos and continued in its orbit around Mars until August 1980. The Viking Lander touched

Below: **Photographed during Viking 2's approach, this dramatic color picture of Mars was taken 5 August 1976 from a distance of 260,000 miles (419,000 kilometers). Bright plumes of water-ice clouds shoot from the volcano Ascraeus Mons. On the right is Argyre, one of the largest impact scars on Mars, surrounded by surface frost and fog.**

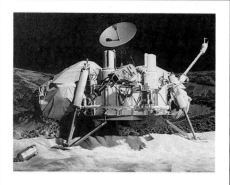

Above: **A mockup of a Viking lander. The Viking missions have transmitted over 52,000 photographs, and increased by at least 20 times our knowledge of Martian geology.**
Below: **Olympus Mons' summit caldera comprises a series of craters formed by repeated collapses after eruptions. The volcano towers over 16 miles (25.6 kilometers) above the Martian surface. By contrast, Mount Everest stands 5.5 miles (9 kilometers) above the Earth's sea level, while Hawaii's Mauna Loa, the largest comparable feature on Earth, rises a mere 5 miles (8 kilometers) above the ocean floor.**

down in the Utopia region on 3 September 1976 and continued to transmit data until April 1980. The Viking 2 Orbiter surveyed the Martian moon Deimos and continued to operate until it was powered down by Earth-based technicians in July 1978.

The Viking project expanded our knowledge of Mars manyfold and returned spectacular close-up photographs of the Martian surface that spanned Mars' seasonal changes for more than a Martian year. Viking answered a great many questions about Mars, but the notion of Martian life remains an enigma.

There were three biology experiments aboard the Viking landers that were specifically designed to detect evidence of Martian life, but the answer returned was a resounding 'maybe not.' In each experiment, samples of Martian soil were scooped up by the landers' remote while 'eating' the 'broth.' To distinguish a chemical reaction from a biological reacdesigned to determine whether Martian organisms

would be able to assimilate and reduce carbon monoxide or carbon dioxide as plants on Earth do. The easily monitored isotope carbon-14 was used and the results were described as 'weakly positive.' While the experiment could not be repeated by Viking on Mars, parallel experiments on Earth showed that the same results could possibly be explained by chemical, rather than biological, reactions.

In the Labeled Release Experiment an organic nutrient 'broth' was prepared and 'fed' to some samples of Martian soil, again using carbon-14 as the trace element. If microorganisms were present, they would 'breathe out' carbon dioxide as they 'ate' the nutrients. Carbon dioxide was, in fact, detected! However, the outgassing of carbon dioxide stopped and could not be restarted. This could have indicated some sort of chemical reaction or that a microbe *had* been present, but that it had died while 'eating' the 'broth.' To distinguish a chemical reaction from a biological reac-

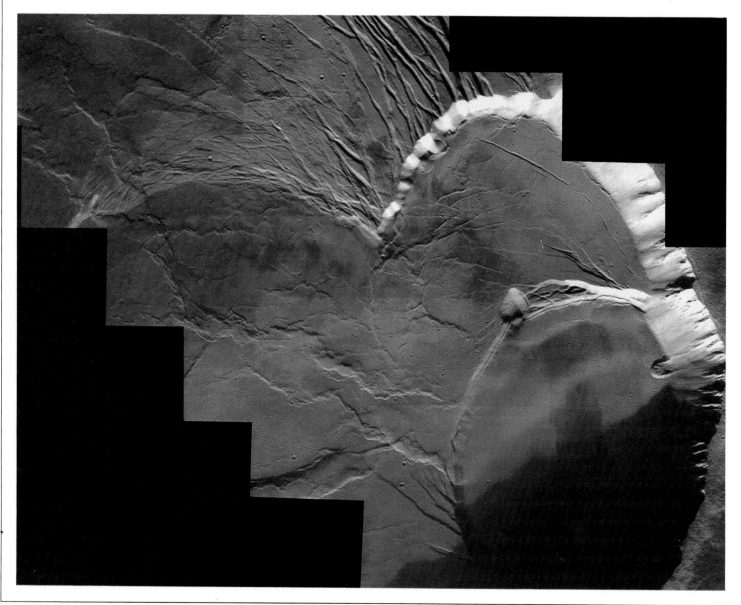

tion, the mixture was heated. This process stopped whatever it was that was producing the carbon dioxide, which *should* have ruled against the notion of a chemical reaction, but which might confirm that it had been caused by a now-deceased organism. In the end, the Labeled Release Experiment was labeled 'inconclusive' because the activities of whatever produced the carbon dioxide had no exact parallel with known reactions of Earth life.

The Gas Exchange Experiment was designed to examine Martian soil samples for evidence of gaseous metabolic changes, by again mixing a sample with a nutrient 'broth.' Because the Martian environment is so dry, it was decided to gradually humidify the samples before plunging them into the 'broth' so as not to 'shock' any of the life forms that might be present. A major shock came instead to the Earth-based experimenters as the sample was being humidified—there was a sudden burst of oxygen! When the nutrient 'broth' itself was added, there was some evidence of carbon dioxide but no more oxygen. Once again the results were described as 'inconclusive' because the results could not be explained by known biological reactions. Subsequent studies have been done to attempt to determine whether some type of oxidizing agent exists in the Martian soil which could provide a 'chemical reaction' explanation of the strange results of the Gas Exchange Experiment.

The three Viking biology experiments raised some curious questions, but there remain no conclusive answers to the question that has intrigued Earth-bound observers. Perhaps the answer lies closer to the Martian poles where there is more water, or perhaps the question might be restated as whether life *might have existed* at one time on Mars. In the long-gone days when rivers ran on the Martian surface, did some civilization, or even just a moss, flourish on their banks? Will paleontologists or archaeologists from Earth one day discover fossils or ruins amid the drifting rust-red Martian sands?

Above: A combination of dust particles, solid water and frozen carbon dioxide is heavy enough to settle to the Martian surface. This ice is perhaps no more than one-thousandth of an inch thick.
Below: Argyre, the smooth plain surrounded by heavily cratered terrain, is a large impact basin that has been observed from Earth for many years. Above the horizon are layers of haze thought to be frozen crystals of carbon dioxide.

MARTIAN MOONS

bserving Mars from the US Naval Observatory in Washington, DC, the American astronomer Asaph Hall (1829-1907) determined that the red planet was accompanied by two tiny moons. Named Deimos (terror) and Phobos (fear) after the characteristics of (some sources say 'the horses of') the Roman war god Mars, the two moons are irregularly shaped rocks pocked with numerous craters. Phobos, the larger of the pair, is just over 17 miles in length, while Deimos is less than nine miles long. Because of their shape, size and texture, it is thought that they originated among the asteroids and became trapped in Martian orbit at the time of the formation of the Solar System. Neither

Below: **Viking 1 Orbiter flew within 300 miles (480 miles) of Mars' inner satellite, Phobos, to obtain the pictures in this mosaic of the asteroid-size moon.**

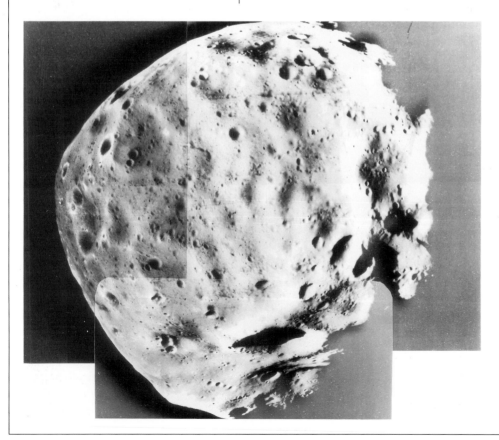

Deimos nor Phobos have the mass to allow them to hold an atmosphere, but they exert sufficient gravity to retain a thin layer of dust on their surfaces—which is perhaps residue from the meteorite impacts that caused the cratering.

Deimos and Phobos are relatively small, and the former would appear no larger from the Martian surface than Venus does from the Earth. Phobos, however, would appear as if it were one third the size of the Earth's Moon. Though both moons revolve around Mars in the same direction, Phobos would *appear* to revolve in the *opposite* direction because it revolves in less than eight hours, a third of the time that it takes Mars to rotate on its axis.

Phobos has a number of large craters, the largest of which, Stickney, is six miles across, while the average Phobos crater diameter is about 500 feet. Other features include fractures that were probably induced by Martian gravitational effects.

Deimos has a much smoother surface than its larger brother, with fewer craters and none with diameters greater than two miles.

THE ASTEROIDS

While their name translates as implying a star-like character, asteroids are more accurately described as planetoids or minor planets. Literally they are fragments of rock that may have their origin in the cataclysmic destruction of one or several terrestrial planets, or they may be debris left over from the origin of the Solar System itself. The largest asteroid, Ceres, is 485 miles in diameter, but there are only six known asteroids with diameters greater than 100 miles.

The discovery of the field of minor planets in the 342 million mile interval between the orbits of Mars and Jupiter that we know as the Asteroid Belt dates to the theoretical work of German astronomer Johann Elert Bode (1747-1826) of the Berlin Observatory. In 1772 Bode authored Bode's Law, which took into account the regular intervals between the known planets and postulated that a planet should, by his law, exist between Mars and Jupiter. Little did Bode realize that this interval was not filled by a single planet, but rather by thousands of planetoids.

In 1800 Bode's countryman Johann Hieronymus Schroeter (1745-1816) organized what he called the Celestial Police, an association of astronomers dedicated to finding the planet whose existence had been postulated by Bode (and by Titius of Wittenberg before him). Ironically, the first, and largest, asteroid, Ceres, was not discovered by a member of Schroeter's Celestial Police, but was discovered on New Year's Day in 1801 by Giuseppe Piazzi (1746-1826), director of the observatory at Palermo, Sicily. Though Piazzi later joined the Celestial Police, the most successful member was Heinrich Olbers (1748-1840), a German amateur astronomer who was able to 'recover,' or rediscover, Ceres in 1802.

Olbers then went on to discover the asteroids Pallas and Vesta in 1802 and 1807 respectively. It would be over 30 years, however, before a fifth asteroid would be discovered.

In 1830 another German amateur astronomer, Karl Ludwig Hencke (1793-1866), went on a search for further asteroids which finally bore fruit in 1845 with the discovery of Astraea. By the 1840s photography was brought into play as a tool and suddenly the search for new asteroids took on a whole new flavor. Both Iris and Flora were discovered in 1847, the same year that Hencke found Hebe, and after that several were found each year. Within ten years, 48 asteroids had been discovered, and by 1899 there were 451 known asteroids. By 1930, the year that Clyde Tombaugh discovered Pluto, there were more than 1000 known asteroids. After World War II the International Astronomical Union set up a cooperative program of asteroid research. By 1980 there were more than 2000 known asteroids, and by the end of 1990 the number exceeded 3500.

The Largest Asteroids

	diameter
Ceres	622 mi (1003 km)
Pallas	377 mi (608 km)
Vesta	334 mi (538 km)
Hygeia	279 mi (450 km)
Euphrosyne	229 mi (370 km)
Interamnia	217 mi (350 km)
Davida	200 mi (323 km)
Cybele	192 mi (309 km)
Europa	180 mi (280 km)
Patienta	171 mi (276 km)
Eunomia	169 mi (272 km)
Doris	155 mi (250 km)
Psyche	155 mi (250 km)
Undina	155 mi (250 km)
Bamberga	153 mi (246 km)
Themis	145 mi (234 km)
Arethusa	143 mi (230 km)

JUPITER

When the Solar System was being formed 4.6 billion years ago, Jupiter may have had the makings of becoming a star. At that time it was 10 times its present diameter and heated by gravitational contraction. It may have blazed like a second Sun.

Had the nuclear reactions within Jupiter become self sustaining as they did in the Sun, the two objects may have become a double star of the type that exists elsewhere in the galaxy and the Solar System would have been a vastly different place than it is today. However, Jupiter failed as a star and gradually began to cool and to collapse to its present size. As Jupiter cooled it became less brilliant, so that after a million years the

Above: **Jupiter and Ganymede, the largest planet and the largest moon in the Solar System.**
Opposite: **Voyager 2 witnessing a sunrise over the horizon of Jupiter.**

'star that might have been' went from one hundred thousandth the luminosity of the Sun to one ten billionth. Today, as much energy is still radiated from *within Jupiter itself* as it *receives from the Sun*.

Named for the king of all the Roman gods, Jupiter is the largest planet in the Solar System, and second in mass only to the Sun. This 'king' of planets has 1330 times the volume of the Earth and 318 times the mass.

Like the Sun, Jupiter is composed almost entirely of hydrogen and helium and, unlike the terrestrial planets, it may be composed almost entirely of gases and fluids with no solid surface. If there is a solid rocky surface, the solid diameter of Jupiter may actually be just slightly larger than the Earth. Above this rocky surface, if it exists, there may be a layer of ice more than 4000 miles thick which is kept frozen by *pressure* rather than temperature, as the *temperatures* would be frightfully hot.

Jupiter's magnetic field is more than 4000 times greater than that of the Earth, leading observers to postulate the existence of a metallic core. Strangely, the center of Jupiter's magnetic field is not located at the planet's center, but at a point 6200 miles offset from the center and tipped by 11 degrees from the rotational axis. This point is also the center of Jupiter's vast magnetosphere, which is six million miles across. Three million miles from Jupiter, the plasma reaches the hottest temperatures recorded in the Solar System, roughly 17 times as hot as the interior of the Sun.

There is almost certainly a sea of liquid metallic hydrogen that makes up the bulk of Jupiter. Above the liquid metallic hydrogen is a transitional zone leading to a layer of fluid molecular hydrogen. Jupiter's atmosphere is characterized by colorful swirling clouds that cover the planet completely. These clouds form in Jupiter's troposphere, at the altitude where convection takes place. The lower clouds, like those of the Earth, are thought to be composed of water vapor, with

Below: **Jupiter and three of its largest satellites: Io, bright brown-yellow against Jupiter's banded surface; Europa, to the right of Jupiter; and the darkest satellite, Callisto, barely visible at the bottom left of the photograph.**
Opposite: **From Jupiter's equator to the southern polar latitudes is the neighborhood of the Great Red Spot.**

ice crystals being present at higher altitudes. Above these, higher clouds are composed of ammonium hydrosulfide, with Jupiter's high cirrus composed of ammonia. At a point 40 miles above the ammonia cirrus, where the Jovian troposphere gives way to the stratosphere, temperatures can dip to colder than −150 degrees Fahrenheit. Above that, in the ionosphere, however, temperatures increase again.

Jupiter's atmosphere is a complex and dynamic feature characterized by distinct horizontal 'belts,' or darker bands of clouds, that exist at semi-symmetrical intervals in the northern and southern hemispheres, and which alternate with lighter colored 'zones.'

The most outstanding feature on Jupiter is certainly the Great Red Spot. First observed in 1664 by the astronomer Robert Hooke (1653-1703), it is a brick red cloud three times the size of the Earth. Described as a high pressure system, the Great Red Spot resembles a storm and exists at a higher and colder altitude than most of Jupiter's cloud cover, although traces of ammonia cirrus are occasionally observed above it. It rotates in a counterclockwise direction, making a complete rotation every six Earth days, and it varies slightly in latitude. The Great Red Spot is

almost certainly the top of some sort of high altitude updraft plume from below the Jovian cloud cover, but the exact nature of the Great Red Spot is uncertain. One theory is that it is above an updraft in the Jovian atmospheres in which phosphene, a hydrogen-phosphorus compound, rises to high altitudes—where it is broken down into hydrogen and red phosphorus-4 by solar ultraviolet radiation. The pure phosphorus would give the Great Red Spot its characteristic color. Another theory has the Great Red Spot as the top of a column of stagnant air that exists above a topographical surface feature far below, within Jupiter.

The Great Red Spot may be an awesome feature, but it is a transient one. Any storm that has been raging for more than 300 years can certainly be termed as an impressive meteorological phenomenon, but it hasn't been constant in its intensity. Between 1878 and 1882 it was seen as very prominent, but thereafter it dimmed markedly until 1891. Since then, it has waned slightly several times—in 1928, 1938, and again in 1977.

Other intriguing meteorological phenomena have also been observed in the Jovian atmosphere, including smaller red spots in the northern hemisphere and some dark brown features that formed at the same latitude as the Great Red Spot. Designated as the South Tropical Disturbance, these features were first observed in 1900, overtook and 'leaped' past the Great Red Spot several times and gradually began to fade in 1935, disappearing five years later. In 1939 a group of large white spots formed near the Great Red Spot in the southern hemisphere. Like their larger red counterpart, they rotate counterclockwise. Similar but smaller features have been observed in the northern hemisphere, where they are seen to rotate in a clockwise direction.

Jupiter has a distinct ring system that was unknown before the close-up observations by two American Voyager spacecraft in 1979. Unlike Saturn's rings, Jupiter's rings are very thin and narrow, and are not visible except when viewed from behind the night side of the planet, when they would be backlighted by the Sun. The ring system is divided into two parts that begin 29,000 miles above Jupiter's cloud tops, although some traces of ring material exist below that altitude. The two parts are a faint band 3100 miles across, feathering into a brighter band 500 miles across. The rings are composed of dark grains of sand and dust and are probably not more than a mile thick.

JUPITER'S MOONS

Below: Jupiter and its four planet-sized moons, called the Galilean satellites, were photographed in early March 1979 by Voyager 1 and assembled into this composite picture. The satellites are not to scale but *are* in their relative positions. Io, orange in color (upper left), is nearest Jupiter; next are Europa (center), Ganymede, and Callisto (lower right).

Jupiter's 16 known moons are organized into a very orderly system of *four* dissimilar groups, each comprised of four similar sized moons orbiting in distinctly different planes.

The inner group (except for Amalthea) were discovered during the Voyager project and they all have diameters of less than 200 miles. They all orbit in a plane whose orbital inclination is less than half a degree and they are located less than 140,000 miles from Jupiter. The second group, called 'The Galileans,' were discovered in 1610 by Galileo Galilei (1564-1642) and have diameters greater than 1900 miles. They all orbit in a plane whose orbital inclination is less than half a degree and they are all between 250,000 and 700,000 miles from Jupiter.

The third group were discovered in the twentieth century prior to the Voyager project, and they all have diameters of less than 105 miles. They all orbit in a plane whose orbital inclination is between 26 and 29 degrees, and they all are between 6.9 and 7.2 million miles from Jupiter. Like the third group, the final group were all discovered in the twentieth century prior to the Voyager project, and they all have diameters of less than 17 miles. They all exist in a plane whose orbital inclination is between 147 and 163 degrees and they are all between 12.8 and 14.7 million miles from Jupiter.

The inner group of Jovian moons are dominated by Amalthea, discovered in 1892 by Edward Emerson Barnard (1857-1923). Amalthea is named for the goat-like nurse of Zeus, the Greek equivalent of the Roman god Jupiter. In Greek mythology, Zeus broke off one of Amalthea's horns and endowed it with the power to be filled with anything the owner wished, causing Amalthea to become associated with prosperity and riches. The innermost Jovian moon, Metis is named for the Greek god of prudence, wife of Zeus and mother of Athena. The other two inner Jovian moons, Adrastea and Thebe, were originally designated 1979 Jl and 1979 J2 and were the first two new moons in the Solar System to be discovered by the Voyager project. Adrastea is named for the mythical Greek king of Argos, whose daughter married Polynices of Thebes, who had been exiled by his brother. Adrastea (or Adrastus) led several primitive expeditions against Thebes.

The Galileans, Jupiter's second group of moons, were all discovered by Galileo (hence their name) during the first month (December 1609-January 1610) of the great astronomer's telescopic survey of the heavens. Aside from the Earth's Moon, they were the first planetary satellites to be observed and are easily seen from Earth with a telescope of moderate power. They are not only much, much larger than any other Jovian moons, they are among the largest in the Solar System, and Ganymede is *the* largest moon in the Solar System.

The next group of Jovian moons are Leda, Himalia, Lysithea and Elara. Himalia

THE MOONS OF JUPITER

	Discovery Date	Diameter	Distance from Jupiter
Metis	Project Voyager, 1979	30 mi (49 km)	79,750 mi (127,600 km)
Adrastea	Project Voyager, 1979	21 mi (35 km)	83,030 mi (134,000 km)
Amalthea	Edward Barnard, 1892	103 mi (166 km)	112,655 mi (181,300 km)
Thebe	Project Voyager, 1979	47 mi (75 km)	137,690 mi (222,000 km)
Io	Galileo Galilei, 1610	2257 mi (3632 km)	261,970 mi (421,600 km)
Europa	Galileo Galilei, 1610	1942 mi (3126 km)	416,877 mi (670,900 km)
Ganymede	Galileo Galilei, 1610	3278 mi (5276 km)	664,867 mi (1.1 million km)
Callisto	Galileo Galilei, 1610	2995 mi (4820 km)	1.2 million mi (1.9 million km)
Leda	Charles Kowal, 1974	5 mi (8 km)	6.9 million mi (11.1 million km)
Himalia	CD Perrine, 1904	105 mi (170 km)	7.1 million mi (11.5 million km)
Lysithea	SB Nicholson, 1938	12 mi (19 km)	7.3 million mi (11.7 million km)
Elara	CD Perrine, 1905	50 mi (80 km)	7.3 million mi (11.7 million km)
Ananke	SB Nicholson, 1951	11 mi (17 km)	12.8 million mi (20.7 million km)
Carme	SB Nicholson, 1938	15 mi (24 km)	13.9 million mi (22.4 million km)
Pasiphae	PJ Melotta, 1908	17 mi (27 km)	14.5 million mi (23.3 million km)
Sinope	PJ Melotta, 1914	13 mi (21 km)	14.7 million mi (23.7 million km)

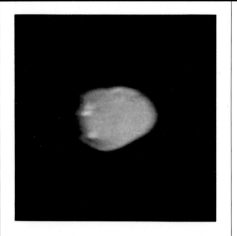

Above: Tiny, red Amalthea, Jupiter's innermost satellite whizzes around the planet every 12 hours. In this view taken by Voyager 1 from a distance of 255,000 miles (425,000 kilometers), the satellite appears about 80 miles (130 kilometers) high by 100 miles (170 kilometers) wide. Amalthea's irregular shape probably results from a long history of impact cratering.

Opposite: Voyager 2 took this picture of Io on 9 July 1979 from 746,000 miles away (1.2 million kilometers). The two blue volcanic eruption plumes are about 62 miles high (100 kilometers) and originate from Amirani (upper) and Maui.

and Elara were discovered by CD Perrine at Lick Observatory between November 1904 and February 1905. Lysithea was discovered by SB Nicholson at Lick Observatory in 1938, while Leda, discovered by Charles Kowal at Mount Palomar in 1974, was the last Jovian moon to be discovered from Earth. Leda is named for the queen of Sparta, who was the mother (by Zeus in the form of a swan) of Helen, Castor and Pollux.

The outermost group of Jovian moons, Ananke, Carme, Pasiphae and Sinope, are the moons most distant from their mother planets of any known in the Solar System. The four moons of the Jovian outer group also all orbit in a *retrograde* motion. The only other moons anywhere in the Solar System that move in retrograde motion are Saturn's Phoebe and Neptune's Triton. SB Nicholson discovered Ananke and Carme with the reflector telescope at Mount Wilson, California in September 1951 and July 1938, respectively. Pasiphae and Sinope were discovered by PJ Melotta at Greenwich, England in January 1908 and July 1914, respectively. Ananke is named for a Greek cult goddess who shared a shrine at Corinth along with the goddess Bia. Horace later assigned her the Latin name Necessitas.

The innermost of Jupiter's Galilean moons, Io, is one of the most intriguing bodies in the Solar System. In 1979 the photographs returned by the two Voyager spacecraft revealed a very dynamic world whose surprising characteristics were beyond anything that had previously been imagined. The most volcanically active body in the Solar System, Io is the only place besides Earth where volcanic eruptions have actually been observed.

Named for the maiden in Greek mythology who became a lover of Zeus only to be turned into a cow by Hera, the moon called Io is a unique world. Io's surface, with its brilliant reds and yellows that remind one of a giant celestial pizza, is a crust of solid sulfur 12 miles thick that floats on a sea of molten sulfur. This sea is, in turn, thought to cover silicate rock which is at least partially molten. The tidal effect of so massive a body as nearby Jupiter is thought to cause the crust to rise and fall on the molten sulfur by as much as sixty miles. It is through this heaving sulfur crust that Io's volcanos have burst.

The red and yellow sulfurous surface is marred by dozens of jet black volcanos whose violent eruptions surpass (both in magnitude and frequency) anything seen on Earth. During its brief encounter with Io

Below: **A global view of Io.**
Opposite: **Surrounding the black volcanic caldera are black fan-shaped features that are the result of liquid sulfur that cools rapidly as it reaches Io's frigid surface. South of Loki the Voyager imaging team discovered a U-shaped molten sulfur lake 125 miles across that had partially crusted over.**

It was detected by its surface crust temperature of about 65 degrees Fahrenheit—compared to the surrounding surface temperature of less than -230 degrees Fahrenheit. This lake has certainly cooled and solidified by now, while other molten sulfur lakes have no doubt formed elsewhere.

in March 1979, Voyager 1 observed the eruptions of no fewer than eight volcanoes, with the plume above Pele reaching an altitude of 174 miles. When Voyager 2 turned its cameras toward Io four months later, it was able to observe eruptions still taking place at all the volcanos discovered by Voyager 1 except two.

In these violent eruptions, sulfurous material is belched from Io's liquid mantle at speeds of up to 3280 feet per second—many times the recorded velocity of the Earth's volcanos. The reason for the altitudes of the plumes and the velocity of the particles is due in part to the weaker gravity on Io—whose mass is less than two percent that of the Earth. The sulfur particles fall to the surface relatively fast, how-

ever, because there is no atmosphere on Io in which they could become suspended, and hence no winds to blow them in great billowing clouds of ash across the land, as was the case on Earth following the recent eruptions of Mount Etna and Mount St Helens.

Each of Io's volcanic eruptions dumps 10,000 tons of sulfur onto the moon's surface. In extrapolation, this would account for 100 billion tons of sulfur deposits per year. This is enough to cover the entire surface with a layer of sulfur 'ash' a foot thick in 30,750 years—a relatively short time, geologically speaking. Combined with surface flows, Io could very well be completely resurfaced with a foot-thick layer in as short a period of time as 3100 years, giving this pizza-colored moon the

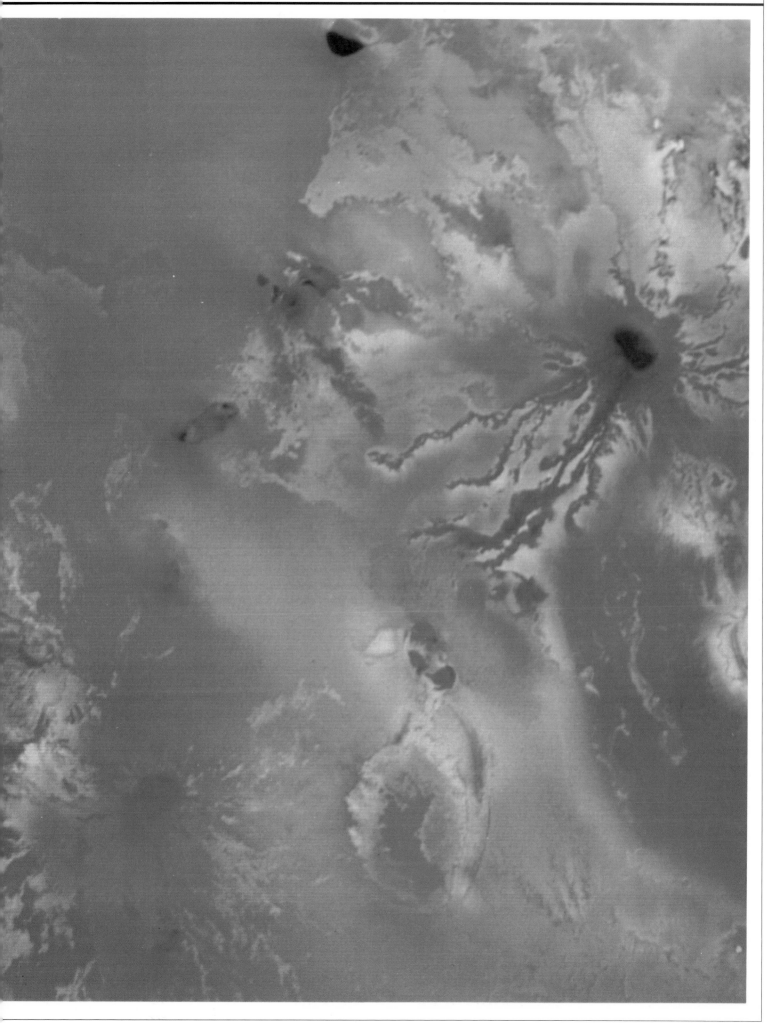

Europa (*right*) is thought to have a relatively large silicate core with a layer of molten silicate above that, which is, in turn, covered by a layer of liquid water perhaps 60 miles deep. Above this is the strange, icy crust, which is roughly 40 miles thick.

Below: **The most unusual features on Europa are the flexus. Light colored, scalloped ridges, the flexus are much narrower and somewhat shorter than the linea. They are, however, more regular in width and in the regularity of their scallops or cusps.**

youngest solid surface in the Solar System aside from Earth, and there are parts of Earth that change *less* over time than does much of Io. In fact, there were many noticeable changes in Io's surface—particularly around the volcano Pele—in just the

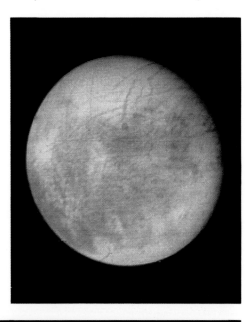

four months between March and July 1979. This 'ever-youthful' surface accounts for the complete absence of meteorite impact craters on Io.

The moon Europa has a surface that is probably composed entirely of water ice. The fact that this surface is marred only by three definite impact craters, Europa is a mystery. The absence of impact craters on Io is explained by its violently active surface, but Europa has an extremely smooth and apparently inactive surface. Named for the Phoenician princess abducted to Crete by Zeus, Europa has a highly reflective surface that probably remained in a slushy semi-liquid state until relatively recently. This is at present the only explanation for its lack of meteorite craters.

The smooth surface is, however, not without features and these, too, present part of Europa's mystery. The features include long black linea, or lines, reminiscent of Percival Lowell's 'canals' on Mars. These features, which are up to 40 miles wide and stretch for thousands of miles across the surface, defy explanation. They appear to be cracks in the lighter surface, but they have no depth and thus they can only be described as 'marks' on the surface.

Ganymede is the largest moon in the Jovian system and is, indeed, the largest moon in the entire Solar System. Ganymede, like Callisto, is composed of silicate rock and water ice, and thus these bodies came to be dubbed 'dirty snowballs.' Named for the cupbearer of the Greek gods, Ganymede has an ice crust that is roughly 60 miles thick. This crust, in turn, floats upon a mantle of slushy, partially-liquid water that is roughly 400 miles deep. Beneath Ganymede's mantle is a heavy silicate core.

Like Earth's rocky crust, Ganymede's icy crust is divided into plates which shift and move independently, interacting with one another along fracture zones, resulting in geologic activity that is very much like what has been observed on Earth. Mountain ranges 10 miles across and 3000 feet high have formed on Ganymede as result of the pressure of ice plates against one another. The surface of Ganymede is characterized by mountainous terrain and ancient dark plains, the largest of which is the region known as Galileo Regio. The dark plains are, in turn, marked by a wrinkled or grooved terrain consisting of a semicircular system of parallel, curved ridges six miles wide, 325 feet high and approximately 40 miles apart. These grooves are the remnants of an ancient impact basin that has long since been obscured by subsequent geologic activity.

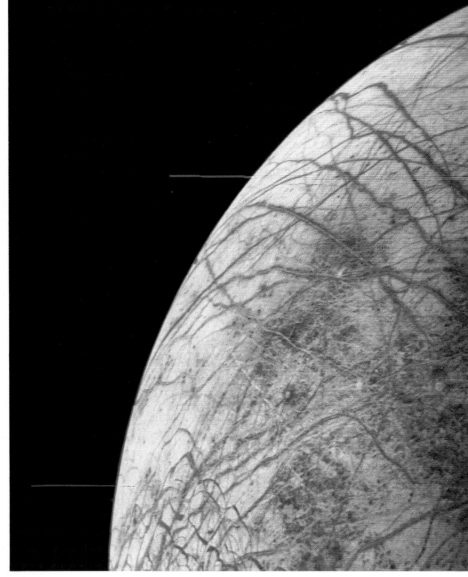

Callisto has a water ice and silicate rock composition like that of Ganymede, but unlike Ganymede, Callisto's ice and silicate soil surface shows no sign of any geologic activity. The only surface feature on this 'dirty snowball' is a mass of hundreds upon hundreds of impact craters. The largest of these is Valhalla, a huge impact basin in Callisto's northern hemisphere that measures 1860 miles across. The probable reason for the lack of geologic activity is that Callisto's icy crust is more than 150 miles thick, and thus is not prone to break into plates as Ganymede's has. It is also much farther from the tidal effects of Jupiter's gravity. Beneath the solid ice crust is a slushy mantle 600 miles in depth, and beneath the mantle is a heavy silicate core. Thus Callisto is thought to be identical to Ganymede in terms of its composition, but with a thicker, and hence more geologically inert, crust.

Callisto was named for a Greek nymph favored by Zeus and turned into a bear by the jealous Hera. With temperatures ranging between −200 and −300 degrees Fahrenheit—roughly the same temperature as Hera's heart—there is little likelihood of an atmosphere hanging over Callisto's frigid wastes.

Above: Callisto as photographed by Voyager from 1.4 million miles. *Left:* Ganymede with the dark Valhalla region evident.

A great number of smaller impact craters have been identified on both Ganymede's and callisto's surfaces, with many of them showing white 'halos.' These are evidence of water having been splashed up through the crust after each fiery meteoroid smashed its way through the surface.

Because of the size of Ganymede and the presence of liquid water, it once was suggested that there might be a tenuous atmosphere of water vapor and free oxygen (with the latter being formed by the effect of sunlight on the former). No evidence of an atmosphere was detected by the Voyager spacecraft in 1979, and indeed, if one were present, it would have to have an atmospheric pressure less than one hundred billionth of Earth's.

SATURN

Opposite: **Voyager 1 caught this unique perspective of Saturn, in which the planet's bright crescent shines through all but the densest of the rings, while the planet's shadow partially obscures them.**

In terms of sheer size, Saturn dwarfs all the other planets except Jupiter, but its incredible system of rings puts it visually in a class by itself. Named for Jupiter's father, the original patriarch of Roman gods, Saturn is the outermost of the planets visible from Earth with the unaided eye.

Saturn's composition is very much like that of Jupiter. There is probably a solid core composed of iron and silicates that measures about 9300 miles in diameter, which is covered by a layer of water kept in solid ice form by the pressure of successive higher layers of metallic hydrogen and liquid molecular hydrogen. Like Jupiter, nearly 80 percent of Saturn's mass is

hydrogen, the simplest element, with most of the remainder taken up by helium, the second simplest and second most common element in the Solar System, so Saturn may have had the same star-like ancestry as Jupiter. Major components of the core are iron (0.2 percent) and silicates (0.1 percent), as well as oxygen (1 percent), which also is present, with hydrogen, in the water ice. The remaining elements are the inert gas neon (0.2 percent) which, along with organic gases composed of nitrogen (0.1 percent) and carbon (0.4 percent), comprise Saturn's atmosphere.

Saturn's atmosphere contains many of the same gases that are present in the atmospheres of Jupiter, Uranus and Neptune. The most common are methane and ammonia, but there are also traces of phosphene and more complex organic compounds such as propane, ethane, acetylene and methylacetylene. Saturn's atmosphere is a good deal smoother, hazier and less

choppy than Jupiter's, with relatively few distinct features to parallel Jupiter's brown, white and 'Great Red' spots.

Saturn's cloud tops are smoother than Jupiter's, and this is probably due to weaker gravity (because of smaller mass) and lower temperatures. At these colder temperatures the condensation point of the chemicals in the atmosphere would be reached in regions of higher pressure and, hence, at lower altitudes within the atmosphere. However, Saturn's atmosphere is probably characterized by the same visible turbulence as Jupiter's, but at lower altitudes below a layer of ammonia haze. Saturn's atmosphere is characterized by horizontal bands alternating between those with westerly—or the rarer easterly—prevailing winds. These winds have speeds of up to 900 mph, with the greatest westerly velocities being recorded within five degrees latitude of the equator. The largest feature in Saturn's atmosphere is

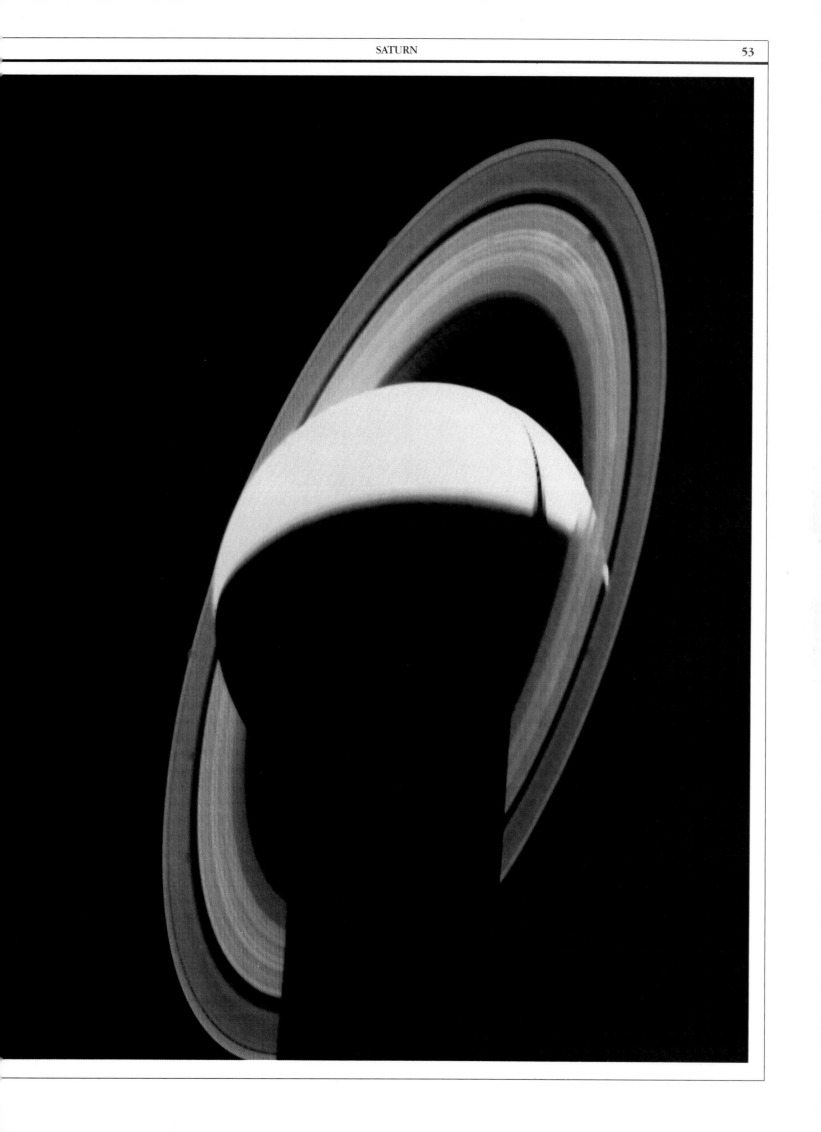

Below: In this Voyager 2 false color print, taken on 11 August 1981, are two of Saturn's satellites: Dione, on the right, and Enceladus.
Opposite: A color-enhanced portrait of Saturn, taken at a distance of 21 million miles (34 million kilometers).
Overleaf: This true color picture, assembled from Voyager 2 images taken on 4 August 1981, shows four of Saturn's moons. They are, in order of distance from the planet: Tethys, Dione, Mimas and Rhea. The shadow of Tethys appears on Saturn's southern hemisphere. Mimas is less evident, appearing as a bright spot above Tethys; Mimas' shadow appears directly above that of Tethys.

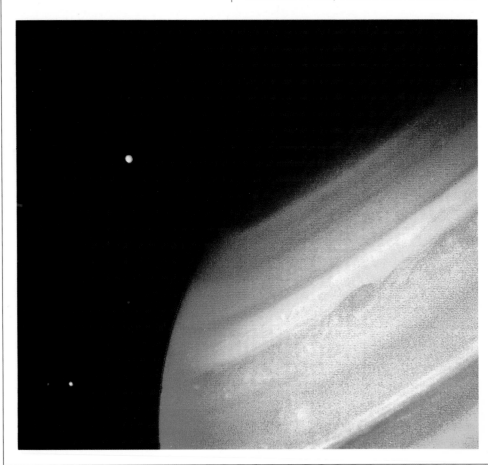

Anne's Spot, a pale red feature in the southern hemisphere that is similar to, though smaller than, Jupiter's Great Red Spot. Like the latter, Anne's Spot is thought to be composed of phosphene that is brought high into the upper atmosphere by spiraling convection currents.

Saturn's ring system, while not absolutely unique, is certainly the planet's outstanding feature. Galileo first observed the rings in 1610, but Saturn happened to be oriented so that the great Italian astronomer was viewing them *nearly* edge-on, and thus it wasn't clear what they were.

Galileo at first thought he had discovered two identical moons of the scale that he had found near Jupiter. However, these 'moons' did not rotate or change position and Galileo was mystified. He wrote to the Grand Duke of Tuscany that 'Saturn is not alone but is composed of three, which almost touch one another and never move nor change with respect to one another. They are arranged in a line parallel to the zodiac, and the middle one [*Saturn itself*] is about three times the size of the lateral ones [*actually the outer edges of the rings*]'.

Two years later the plane of the rings was oriented *directly* at the Earth and the 'lateral moons' seemed to disappear entirely. Galileo was completely baffled, but no less so than when they reappeared in 1613. In December 1612, Galileo had written: 'I do not know what to say in a case so surprising, so unlooked for and so novel. The shortness of the time, the unexpected nature of the event, the weakness of my understanding, and the fear of being mistaken have greatly confounded me.'

More than a decade after Galileo's death in 1655, the Dutch astronomer Christiaan Huygens (1629-1695) solved the riddle. Using a telescope more powerful than that which was available to his predecessor, Huygens figured out that the mysterious objects were rings around Saturn and the reason for their 'disappearance' in 1612. He also went on to calculate that the rings would be oriented in this way on a 150-month cycle, and that at opposing ends of the same cycle almost the entire ring would be visible from Earth. It has since been determined that the cycle actually alternates between periods of 189 and 165 months. Huygens also discovered Saturn's largest moon, Titan.

In 1671 the Italian-born and naturalized French astronomer Giovanni Domenico (aka Jean Dominique) Cassini (1625-1712) began his own observations of the ringed planet. Cassini discovered a second moon of Saturn, Iapetus, in 1671, and in 1675 he determined that the 'ring' around Saturn was not a single band, but a pair of concentric rings. These two rings would come to be known as the A Ring and B Ring, with the space between them appropriately named the Cassini Division. In 1837 Johann Franz Encke (1791-1865) at the Berlin Observatory tentatively identified a faint division in the A Ring. This division was confirmed in 1888 by James Keeler (1857-1900) of the Allegheny Observatory in the United States. Subsequently, this division is known as either the 'Keeler Gap' or (more often) as the 'Encke Division.'

The first manmade spacecraft to venture close to Saturn was the American Pioneer 11 in September 1979. Prior to this time, there were only three known rings of Saturn, each lettered in the order of their discovery from A through C. Pioneer 11 helped Earth-based astronomers identify a fourth ring, which is now known as the F Ring. When the American Voyager 1 Spacecraft first approached Saturn in November 1980, the spectacular photographs that were beamed back to Earth revealed that there were not just four, six, or even a dozen rings in Saturn's ring system; rather, there were literally thousands of rings, with each known ring itself composed of hundreds or thousands of rings, with faint rings identified even within the Cassini Division.

SATURN'S MOONS

Below: Saturn with some of her moons: Dione, Tethys, Mimas, Enceladus, Rhea and Titan.

Not only do its spectacular rings set Saturn apart from other planets, but so too does its complex system of more than 20 moons. Saturn's moons range in size from huge Titan, once thought to be the Solar System's largest moon, to the family of tiny moons that were discovered in photographs taken by the Voyager Spacecraft in 1980. Though the moons of Saturn are no less diverse in character than those of Jupiter, they are generally smaller and, with the exception of the two outermost (Iapetus and Phoebe), their orbital inclinations are within 1.5 degrees of that of the rings. With the exception of Phoebe, the moons are synchronous, like Earth's moon, meaning that the

same side faces Saturn at all times. The western hemispheres, which face in the direction of their orbital paths, are called leading hemispheres, while the eastern are called trailing hemispheres.

In 1977, when the two Voyager Spacecraft were launched from Earth, the ringed planet was known to have nine moons. Five of these were discovered prior to 1700 (with four found by Giovanni Cassini, the man who discovered that Saturn had multiple rings), and only two were discovered after 1800. By the time that the Voyager data was digested in 1982, Saturn was known to have 17 moons and four to six additional Lagrangian co-orbital satellites. A co-orbital is one of a group of moons that share a single orbital path, while Lagrangian satellites (named after the eighteenth century astronomer whose mathematical theory postulated their existence) are small co-orbitals that exist in the orbit of a larger moon and remain 60 degrees ahead or 60 degrees behind it in the orbital path. Saturn's most recently discovered moons are so small and so close to the planet that it is almost hard to know where to draw the line between moons and ring particles. This also makes it harder to find such bodies visually against the brilliant rings.

The innermost of Saturn's moons is Atlas, which is named for one of the Titans of Greek mythology who was condemned to support the weight of the universe on his shoulders. Atlas is also informally known as

the A Ring Shepherd Moon because of its role in shepherding the nearby outer A Ring particles and, in a sense, *defining* the outer edge of the A Ring. The next two moons, Prometheus and Pandora are named respectively for the Titan of Greek mythology who stole fire from Olympus to give it to man, and for the woman who was bestowed upon man as a punishment for Prometheus having stolen fire. Prometheus and Pandora are known informally as F Ring Shepherd Moons because of their positions on either side of the F Ring and

THE MOONS OF SATURN

	Discovery Date	*Diameter*	*Distance from Saturn*
Atlas	Project Voyager, 1980	19 mi (30 km)	85,544 mi (137,670 km)
Prometheus	Project Voyager, 1980	137 mi (220 km)	86,589 mi (139,353 km)
Pandora	Project Voyager, 1980	56 mi (90 km)	88,048 mi (141,700 km)
Epimetheus	Project Voyager, 1980	40 mi (65 km)	94,089 mi (151,422 km)
Janus	Project Voyager, 1980	60 mi (95 km)	94,120 mi (151,472 km)
Mimas	William Herschel, 1789	242 mi (390 km)	115,326 mi (185,600 km)
Enceladus	William Herschel, 1789	311 mi (500 km)	147,948 mi (238,100 km)
Tethys	Giovanni Cassini, 1684	652 mi (1050 km)	182,714 mi (292,342 km)
Telesto	Project Voyager, 1980	9 mi (15 km)	183,118 mi (294,700 km)
Calypso	Project Voyager, 1980	9 mi (15 km)	217,480 mi (350,000 km)
Dione	Giovanni Cassini, 1684	696 mi (1120 km)	234,567 mi (377,500 km)
Helene	Project Voyager, 1980	20 mi (32 km)	234,915 mi (378,060 km)
Rhea	Giovanni Cassini, 1672	951 mi (1530 km)	327,586 mi (527,200 km)
Titan	Christiaan Huygens, 1655	3200 mi (5150 km)	759,067 mi (1.2 million km)
Hyperion	GP Bond and William Lassell, 1848	155 mi (250 km)	921,493 mi (1.5 million km)
Iapetus	Giovanni Cassini, 1671	905 mi (1460 km)	2.2 million mi (3.6 million km)
Phoebe	William Pickering, 1898	137 mi (220 km)	8 million mi (13 million km)

Right: Discovered in 1789 by the German-born, but naturalized English, astronomer William Herschel (1738-1822), Mimas is scarred by a huge impact crater that bears his name. The walls of the crater Herschel average 16,000 feet, and a huge mountain at the crater's center rises nearly 20,000 feet from its crater floor. This huge crater is centered precisely on the equator and has a diameter one third the diameter of Mimas itself.

Right: The second largest of Saturn's moons, Rhea was discovered by Giovanni Cassini (1625-1712) in 1672 and was named for the wife of Kronos, who according to Greek mythology, ruled the universe until dethroned by his son Zeus. In Roman mythology, as well as in astronomical nomenclature, Rhea is identified with Saturn because Saturn is the father of Jupiter, the Roman equivalent of Zeus.

Below: Enceladus is named for the giant who rebelled against the gods of Greek mythology, and who was subsequently struck down and buried on Mount Etna. Discovered by William Herschel (1738-1822) in 1789 at the same time that he identified Mimas, Enceladus is the most geologically active of Saturn's moons.

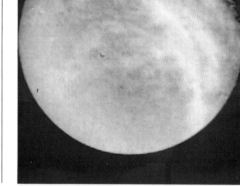

their role in defining that ring. The two moons may also be responsible for the kinks and braiding observed in the F Ring.

Well beyond the F Ring, but inside of the G Ring, are Epimetheus and Janus, which are the first of the several groups of co-orbital moons and the only group of co-orbitals not to be of the Lagrangian type. The centers of these two bodies, and hence the 'center lines' of their orbital paths, are offset by only 30 miles, a distance narrower than the radius of either! Epimetheus is named for the brother, in Greek mythology, of Prometheus, who accepted Pandora (a gift from Zeus) as his wife, despite the warning of his brother. As Prometheus had warned, Pandora opened the infamous box, releasing all the evils within. Janus, the two-faced Roman god of doorways, became the namesake of a moon that was thought to have been identified in 1966 at distance of 105,000 miles from Saturn. The existence of this 'first' Janus was disproven, but the name was reassigned to 1980 S26, which was discovered in a nearby orbit.

Larger than either of the planets Mercury and Pluto, Titan is the second largest moon in the Solar System (after Ganymede). Once thought to be the largest, it was named for the family of pre-Olympian Greek gods whose name implies colossal size. Titan was discovered by the Dutch astronomer Christiaan Huygens in 1655, making it one of the first moons to be discovered in the Solar System. Though no longer on the throne as the Solar System's largest moon, it certainly must rank as one of the most spectacular.

Titan is the only known moon with a fully developed atmosphere that consists of more than simply trace gases. It has, in fact, a denser atmosphere and cloud cover than either Earth or Mars. This cloud cover, nearly as opaque as that which shrouds Venus, has prevented the sort of surface mapping that has been possible with the other major moons of the outer Solar System, but its presence has only served to make Titan all that much more intriguing. (Early astronomers mistook this dense atmosphere for Titan's actual surface, and it was through this mistake that Titan was once considered to be the Solar System's largest moon.)

Why Titan was able to develop an atmosphere, while Ganymede and Callisto (bodies of similar size) did not, is a matter of conjecture. It has been theorized that all the Solar System's largest moons had similar chemistry in the beginning, but Titan evolved in a colder part of the Solar System—farther away from the Sun and from

Jupiter—when it almost became a primordial star. Thus the hydrocarbon gases were able to exist as solids on Titan, while the gases of Jupiter's Galilean moons dissipated into space, leaving only water and rock. Saturn's other moons meanwhile, were never large enough to have sufficient gravity to hold an atmosphere.

The presence of nitrogen, a hydrocarbon atmosphere and water indicate that Titan's surface is very much like that of the Earth four billion years ago before life evolved on the latter body. It has been suggested that this similarity to the prebiotic 'soup' that covered the Earth in those bygone days could presage a similar chain of events on Titan.

The view from Titan's surface is one of an exciting, but inhospitable, world. Covered by the opaque haze, the sky would appear like a smoggy sunset on Earth or like a view from the surface of Venus. The atmospheric pressure on on Titan's surface, while 1.6 times that of Earth is, however, a good deal less than that of Venus. Titan's surface temperature of nearly 300 degrees Fahrenheit would permit methane to exist not only as a gas, but also as a liquid or a solid, in much the same way that water does on Earth. A picture is thus painted of a cold, orange-tinted land where methane rain or snow falls from the methane clouds and where methane rivers may flow into methane oceans dotted with methane icebergs. There is evidence of a 30 Earth-year seasonal cycle which *may* have permitted the development of methane ice caps that expand and recede like the water ice caps on Earth (and the water/carbon dioxide ice caps on Mars). Water ice is also present on Titan, beneath the methane surface features, and possibly extends up into the atmosphere in the form of ice mountains. Titan's mantle is, in turn, largely composed of water ice that gives way to a rocky core perhaps 600 miles beneath the surface. The absence of a magnetic field indicates that Titan has no significant amount of ferrous metallic minerals in its core.

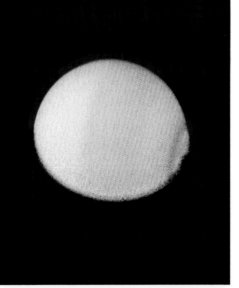

Left: The most notable feature on Tethys is the mysterious Ithaca Chasma, an enormous rift canyon that runs from near the north pole all the way to the south pole. With an average width of 60 miles and an average depth of three miles, Ithaca Chasma dwarfs the Earth's Grand Canyon in both scale and absolute terms. In the scale of the Earth, the equivalent of Ithaca Chasma would be like having a 40-mile deep trench as wide as the state of Colorado, extending from Nome, Alaska, to the southern tip of Argentina.

Left: Titan's atmosphere is extremely rich in nitrogen, the same element that makes up the greatest part of the Earth's atmosphere. Other major components of Titan's atmosphere are hydrocarbon gases, such as acetylene, ethane and propane, with methane being the most common of the hydrocarbons.

Below: Dione's surface is darker than any of Saturn's other ice/rock moons, indicating that there are large regions of exposed rock. Dione's surface is characterized by impact craters common to both icy and rocky surface areas. The craters are generally smaller than 25 miles across, but Amata, the largest, measures nearly 150 miles in diameter.

Below Left: Tiny, distant Iapetua.

URANUS

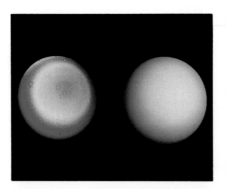

Above: **Voyager 2 returned this true color image of Uranus on 17 January 1986. Note the blue-green color of Uranus' deep, cold and remarkably clear atmosphere. The darker shadings at the upper right of the disk correspond to the day-night boundary on the planet. Beyond this boundary lies the northern hemisphere of Uranus that remains in total darkness as the planet rotates.**

Uranus is named for the earliest supreme god of Greek mythology. The personification of the sky, mythical Uranus was both son and consort to the goddess Gaea and father of all the Cyclopes and Titans. The first outer Solar System planet to be correctly identified as such in historical times, Uranus was identified in 1781 by the German-born English astronomer William Herschel while he was working at Bath.

Uranus has an axial inclination of 98 degrees, a phenomenon that is unique in the Solar System. With such an axial inclination, Uranus is seen as rotating 'on its side' at a near right angle to the inclination of the Earth or Sun. The poles of Uranus, rather than its equatorial regions, are pointing alternately at the Sun.

Like Jupiter, Saturn and Neptune, Uranus is a gaseous planet with a distinct blue-green appearance, probably due to a concentration of methane in its upper atmosphere. In terms of size, it is smaller than Jupiter and Saturn, while being very close to the size of Neptune. Its solid core is composed of metals and silicate rock with a diameter of roughly 270,000 miles. Its core is, in turn, covered by an icy mantle of methane ammonia and water ice 6000 miles deep.

As with the other gaseous planets, the predominant elements in the Uranian atmosphere are hydrogen and helium, although the Voyager 2 observations in 1986 indicated that the atmosphere was only 15 percent helium, versus 40 percent, as originally postulated. Other atmospheric constituents include methane, acetylene and other hydrocarbons. The clouds that form in this atmosphere are moved by prevailing winds that blow in the same direction as the planet rotates, just as they do on Jupiter, Saturn and Earth. The lowest temperature (-366 degrees Fahrenheit) is recorded at the boundary between troposphere and stratosphere. The coldest latitudes seem to be those between 15 and 40 degrees, but surprisingly, both the poles show similar temperatures whether or not they are sunlit!

Prior to the flyby of Voyager 2 in January 1986, Uranus was thought not to have a magnetic field, but this assumption proved false. The magnetic field of Uranus is tilted at a 60 degree angle to the planet's rotational axis (compared to 12 degrees on Earth). The magnetic field has roughly the same intensity as the Earth's, but whereas the Earth's magnetic field is generated by a molten metallic core, the one surrounding Uranus seems to be generated by the electrically conductive, super pressurized ocean of ammonia and water that exists beneath the atmosphere.

Uranus, like Jupiter and Saturn, has a system of rings, of which the first nine were discovered by Earth-based observers in 1977. In 1986 Voyager 2 observed these in detail and identified two more. This ring system is much more complex than that of Jupiter, but less so than Saturn's spectacular system. The system around Uranus seems to be relatively young and probably did not form at the same time as the planet. The

particles that make up the rings may be the remnants of a moon that was broken by a high velocity impact or torn apart by gravitational effects of Uranus. The widest ring known before Voyager 2 was the outermost ring, Epsilon — an irregular ring measuring 14 to 60 miles across. The outer edge of the system, the outer edge of the Epsilon ring, is sharply defined and is located 15,800 miles from the Uranus cloud tops. At this point the Epsilon Ring is just 500 feet thick, and surprisingly devoid of fragments with diameters below one foot.

Below: Voyager 2 was about 600,000 miles (960,000 kilometers) from Uranus when it acquired this wide angle view of Uranus on 25 January 1986.

Even at this extreme angle, Uranus retains the pale blue-green color seen by ground-based astronomers and recorded by Voyager on its historic encounter. The color results from the methane in the atmosphere which absorbs the red wavelengths of sunlight. The whiteness at the edge of the crescent is due to high-altitude haze.

URANIAN MOONS

Below left: Like the other Uranian moons, Oberon is composed of roughly 50 percent water ice, 30 percent silicate rock, and 20 percent methane-related carbon/nitrogen compounds. Unlike those of the others, however, Oberon's ancient, heavily cratered surface shows very little evidence of internal geological activity. Being the second largest and most massive of the Uranian moons, as well as the farthest from the mother planet, Oberon is the moon least influenced by the tidal effects of the gravity of Uranus.

Far right: While the surfaces of all the Uranian moons are darkened by the presence of methane ice, Umbriel is the darkest. Even its impact craters, which should theoretically show lighter-colored water ice in their bottoms, are dark. Nevertheless, Umbriel is thought to be composed mostly of water ice, with the balance made up of silicate rock and methane ice. As such, Umbriel is like the other Uranian moons, but it just carries most of its methane ice on its surface. Overall, it is the least geologically active of the Uranian moons. Discovered in 1851 by William Lassell (1799-1880) at the same time that he identified Ariel, Umbriel is named for the dusky sprite in Alexander Pope's *The Rape of the Lock.*

Prior to the observations by Voyager 2, Uranus was known to have just five moons. Photographs returned by the spacecraft increased the number of known moons to 15, with all 10 of the newly-discovered moons located *within* the orbital paths of the original five. One of the new moons, Puck, was discovered by Voyager's cameras in late 1985, and the rest were discovered in the photos taken during the January 1986 Voyager flyby of the Uranian system. With the exception of Puck and Cordelia—the largest and smallest of the 'Voyager' moons—all of the newly discovered members of the group are very uniform in size, with diameters ranging between 31 and 37 miles.

The innermost of the moons are Cordelia, located between the Delta Ring and the Epsilon Ring, and Ophelia on the opposite side of the Epsilon. Thus straddling the Epsilon Ring, these two small bodies probably act like the shepherd moons of Saturn, controlling and defining the position and shape of the ring.

Far left: Ariel is largely devoid of impact craters with diameters in excess of 30 miles and has the brightest surface of any of the Uranian moons. Ariel also appears to have undergone a period of intense geologic activity, which has produced many fault canyons and has resulted in many outflows of water ice from the interior.

Left: Miranda's composition is about half water ice, with the balance being divided between silicate rock and methane-related organic compounds. On its surface there are huge fault canyons 12 miles deep and evidence of intense geologic activity. It has been much more geologically active than the other Uranian moons.

THE MOONS OF URANUS

	Discovery Date	Diameter	Distance from Uranus
Cordelia	Project Voyager, 1986	25 mi (40 km)	30,882 mi (49,700 km)
Ophelia	Project Voyager, 1986	31 mi (50 km)	33,429 mi (53,800 km)
Bianca	Project Voyager, 1986	31 mi (50 km)	36,785 mi (59,200 km)
Juliet	Project Voyager, 1986	37 mi (60 km)	38,400mi (61,800 km)
Desdemona	Project Voyager, 1986	37 mi (60 km)	38,959 mi (62,700 km)
Rosalind	Project Voyager, 1986	50 mi (80 km)	40,140 mi 64,600 km)
Portia	Project Voyager, 1986	50 mi (80 km)	41,072 mi (66,100 km)
Cressida	Project Voyager, 1986	37 mi (60 km)	43,433 mi (69,900 km)
Belinda	Project Voyager, 1986	37 mi (60 km)	46,789 mi (75,300 km)
Puck	Project Voyager, 1985	106 mi (170 km)	53,437 mi (86,000 km)
Miranda	Gerard Kuiper, 1948	217 mi (150 km)	80,716 mi (128,282 km)
Ariel	William Lassell, 1851	721 mi (1160 km)	118,358 mi (190,900 km)
Umbriel	William Lassell, 1851	739 mi (1190 km)	165,284 mi (266,000 km)
Titania	William Herschel, 1787	998 mi (1610 km)	271,104 mi (436,300 km)
Oberon	William Herschel, 1787	961 mi (1550 km)	326,507 mi (583,400 km)

NEPTUNE

Facing page: **Neptune, imaged by Voyager 2 on 23 August 1980. Toward the top of the photo is the Great Dark Spot, a convection storm similar to Jupiter's Great Red Spot, with accompanying methane cirrus clouds. Just below this, the speedy, bright cloud known as 'Scooter,' and below this, the Lesser Dark Spot, a convection storm with a permanent cloud bank over its center.**

Below: **A high resolution color image of Neptune's bright cirrus cloud streaks.**

Located 2.8 billion miles from the Sun, Neptune is three times more distant from the Sun than Saturn and more than half again farther out than Uranus. At this distance, it takes 165 years for Neptune to complete one revolution around the Sun. Like Jupiter, Saturn and Uranus, Neptune is a giant gaseous orb. With a diameter of 30,642 miles, Neptune is a near twin of Uranus and is as close in size to this neighbor as Venus is to the Earth. Like Uranus, Neptune has a longer rotational period—16.3 hours—than Jupiter or Saturn, yet this rotational period is less than that of the terrestrial planets. Neptune also corresponds to Uranus in terms of its physical composition, which consists primarily of hydrogen and helium, with a methane and ammonia atmosphere.

After the discovery of Uranus, it took but 65 years before the existence of an eighth planet was confirmed. Galileo had sighted this object as early as 1613, but it was Johann Galle and Heinrich Ludwig D'Arrest who finally identified it as a planet in 1846. They named it Neptune, after the Roman sea god, because of its pale, sea-green color.

Prior to 1989, very little else was known about Neptune. The Voyager 2 spacecraft, which conducted close-up flybys of Jupiter, Saturn and Uranus in 1979, 1981 and 1986, turned its cameras on Neptune in June 1989 and flew to within 3044 miles of the planet on 25 August. During this short time, mankind's knowledge of Neptune and its moons increased one hundred fold. For example, six moons and four rings were discovered, and the existence was confirmed of a magnetic field tilted 50 degrees from Neptune's rotational axis and offset 6000 miles from the planet's center. The

Facing page: The Great Dark Spot, imaged by Voyager 2 during the spacecraft's transit over the face of Neptune, and 45 hours before its closest approach, 3000 miles 'up and over' the planet's north pole.

Below: This picture of Neptune was produced from images taken through the ultraviolet, violet and green filters of the Voyager 2 wide-angle camera, in order to paint clouds of different altitudes different colors. Deep-lying clouds are masked in the ultraviolet wavelength and appear dark blue. Conversely, clouds positioned at high altitudes are rendered as pinkish. To the naked eye they would also appear white.

temperature of Neptune was determined to be −353 degrees Fahrenheit.

Most notable visually was the discovery of the Great Dark Spot in Neptune's atmosphere. Located at a mean latitude of 22 degrees south and with an overall length of 30 degrees longitude, it is very much analogous to Jupiter's Great Red Spot, both in terms of location and its size relative to the planet.

Like the Great Red Spot, the Great Dark Spot is an elliptical, stormlike feature that rotates in a counterclockwise direction and is probably located *above* the surrounding cloud tops. The Great Dark Spot is encircled by a constantly changing pattern of cirrus clouds and followed in its movement through Neptune's atmosphere by a string of much smaller elliptical storms.

The cirrus clouds are composed of methane crystals and cling to the Great Dark Spot the way cirrus cling to mountain tops on the Earth's islands. The Great Dark

Spot completes a revolution of the planet in 18.3 hours, moving east to west.

To the south of the Great Dark Spot is another bright cloud which was observed by Voyager for the entire duration of the flyby and which was nicknamed 'scooter' because it moves at a much faster relative speed than the Great Dark Spot, causing it to overtake the latter every five days. South of this feature is the Lesser Dark Spot with a permanent cloud bank situated over its center.

Because Jupiter, Saturn and Uranus are all encircled by rings of rocky debris, it was long supposed of Neptune as well, although the planet is much too distant for these to be visible from Earth. It was not until two weeks prior to Voyager 2's closest encounter in August 1989 that the existence of these rings was verified. Because Neptune's rings are very irregular, they appeared at first to be incomplete arcs. It is now known that there are four continuous, albeit thin, rings around the planet.

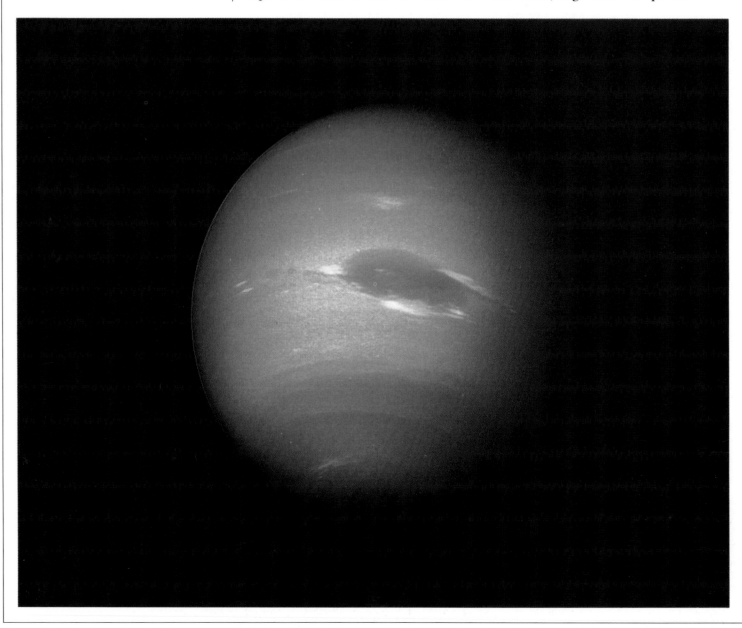

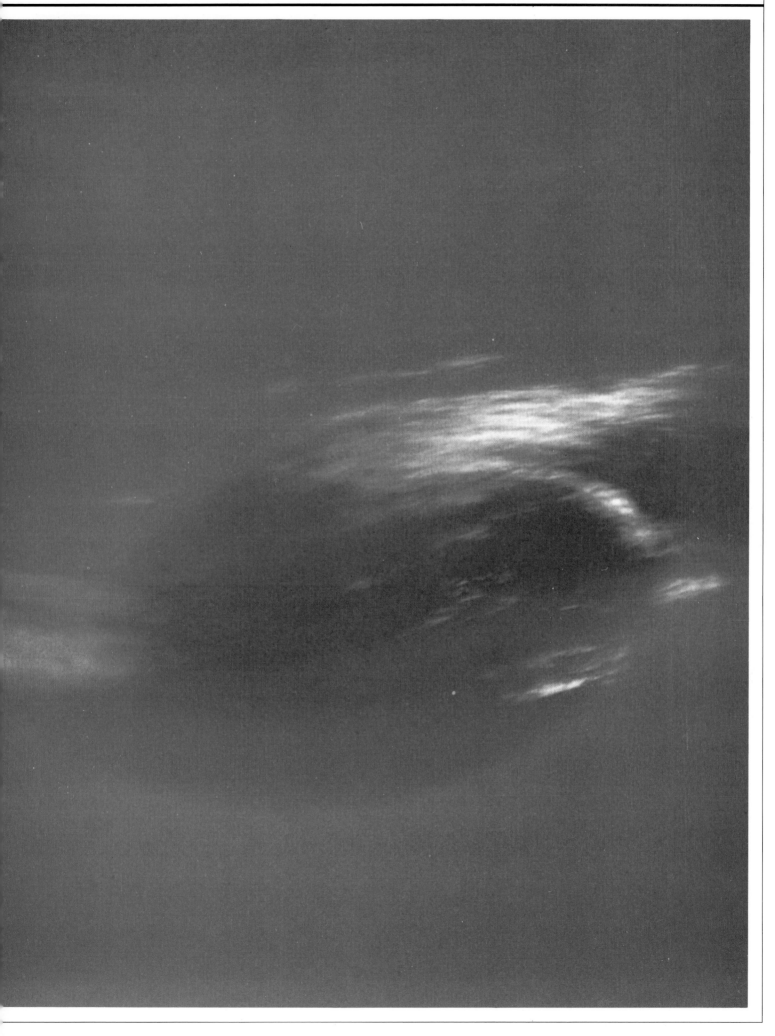

NEPTUNE'S MOONS

Below: **The irregular appearance of Neptune's satellite 1989N2 indicates that this moon, later named Larissa, has remained cold and rigid through much of its history.**
Opposite: **Satellite 1989NI has been named after Proteus, Greek god of the sea.**

Prior to the American Voyager 2 spacecraft encounter with Neptune in 1989, the planet was known to possess two moons, although 1981 observations at the University of Arizona led to a prediction of at least one other moon. Prior to Voyager 2's encounter with Uranus in 1986, only five Uranian moons were known, and Voyager's observations tripled that number. This fact alone would lead us to suspect that Neptune, too, had moons awaiting discovery.

The two Neptunian moons confirmed prior to 1989 are among the most peculiar in the Solar System. Triton, discovered in 1846 less than a month after Neptune, is a huge object with the only retrograde orbit known in the

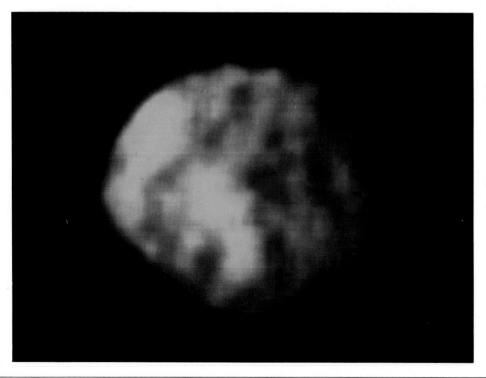

Solar System; while Nereid, discovered more than a century after Triton, has the most elliptical orbit of any known moon in the Solar System. Voyager 2 discovered six additional moons, including the one known as 1989N1 (Proteus), which is actually larger, although darker, than Nereid. This moon is also the largest known nonsymmetrical body in the Solar System.

Triton, which revolves around Neptune in a direction opposite to the mother planet's rotation, was thought to have a diameter of 3700 miles, but which is now known to be 1690 miles. Triton is the second moon in the Solar System (after Saturn's Titan) that has been found to possess an atmosphere. It is a much thinner atmosphere than Titan's but is nevertheless clearly discernible in Voyager 2 photos of Triton's horizon. The atmosphere consists of methane chilled to −400 degrees Fahrenheit, making Triton the coldest object yet observed in the Solar System. Triton

THE MOONS OF NEPTUNE

(NOTE: The numerically designated moons are listed in order of distance,
but numbered in order of discovery.)

	Discovery Date	Diameter	Distance from Neptune
1989N6 (Naiad)	Project Voyager, 1989	30 mi (50 km)	14,400 mi (23,000 km)
1989N5 (Thalassa)	Project Voyager, 1989	60 mi (90 km)	15,500 mi (25,000 km)
1989N3 (Despina)	Project Voyager, 1989	85 mi (135 km)	16,980 mi (27,150 km)
1989N4 (Galatea)	Project Voyager, 1989	100 mi (160 km)	23,180 mi (37,100 km)
1989N2 (Larissa)	Project Voyager, 1989	125 mi (200 km)	30,080 mi (48,100 km)
1989N1 (Proteus)	Project Voyager, 1989	260 mi (420 km)	57,780 mi (92,500 km)
Triton	William Lassell, 1846	1690 mi (2700 km)	205,020 mi (329,880 km)
Nereid	Gerard Kuiper, 1949	300 mi (500 km)	3.4 million mi (5.5 million km)

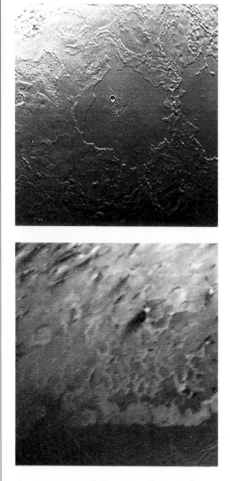

consists primarily of silicate rock, but there is also a great deal of water ice and frozen methane present.

Triton has a very pronounced division between that part of the moon which is experiencing summer and that part which is enduring winter. This phenomenon is not yet explained, nor is the fact that within the 10 years prior to Voyager's flyby, Triton was twice as orange as it appeared both from Earth and from Voyager in August 1989. Evidence of recent volcanic activity on Triton has also been discovered, so that it is now possible to add it to the short list of volcanically active bodies which previously included only the Earth and Jupiter's moon Io.

Triton, Neptune's largest moon, was discovered by English brewer and amateur astronomer William Lassell (1799-1880), just 17 days after the discovery of Neptune itself. Like its parent planet, Triton is named for a god of the sea—in this case, the merman son of the Greek god Poseidon and goddess Amphitrite.

Unique among all the known moons in the Solar System, Triton revolves around its mother planet in the direction opposite to Neptune's rotation. Its orbit is so close to Neptune, and is gradually getting so much closer, that one day Neptune's gravity might pull it apart and scatter it into a Saturn-like ring. (However, if this does happen, it will not be for several million years.) Triton's surface, unlike that of Neptune, is rocky rather than gaseous. This rocky surface is probably covered by methane frost, and, perhaps, a faint methane *atmosphere*.

Nereid, Neptune's second moon, was discovered in 1949 by the Dutch-American astronomer, Gerard Peter Kuiper (1906-1973) in an elliptical orbit far beyond the orbit of Triton. Named for the Nereids—sea nymph daughters of the Greek god Nereis—Nereid is much tinier than its brother Triton. Little is known about Nereid other than its extremely *elliptical* orbit and its size relative to Triton.

At top: **Part of the complex geologic history of icy Triton, Neptune's largest satellite, is shown in this Voyager 2 photograph. Two depressions, possibly old impact basins, have been extensively modified by flooding, melting, faulting and collapse. The rough area in the middle probably marks the most recent eruption of material.**
Above: **A five mile tall geyser was discovered erupting from the surface of Triton by Voyager 2 on 25 August 1989.**
Opposite: **Combining approximately 12 individual images, Voyager 2 created a comprehensive view of the Neptune-facing hemisphere of Triton. The pinkish area is the moon's polar ice cap.**

Near right: **This image of Nereid has sufficient detail to show overall size and albedo (reflecting power) but not surface detail. No spacecraft project is being planned to return to Nereid for a closer look.**
Overleaf: **This dramatic view of the crescents of Neptune and Triton was acquired by Voyager 2 as it plunged southward at an angle of 48 degrees to the plane of the ecliptic. Color was produced through the narrow-angle camera's clear, orange and green filters.**

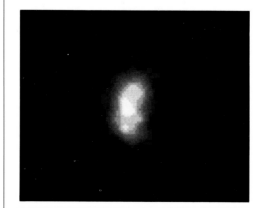

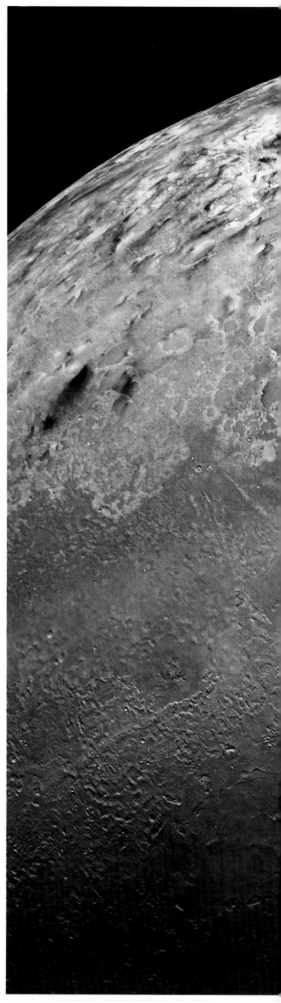

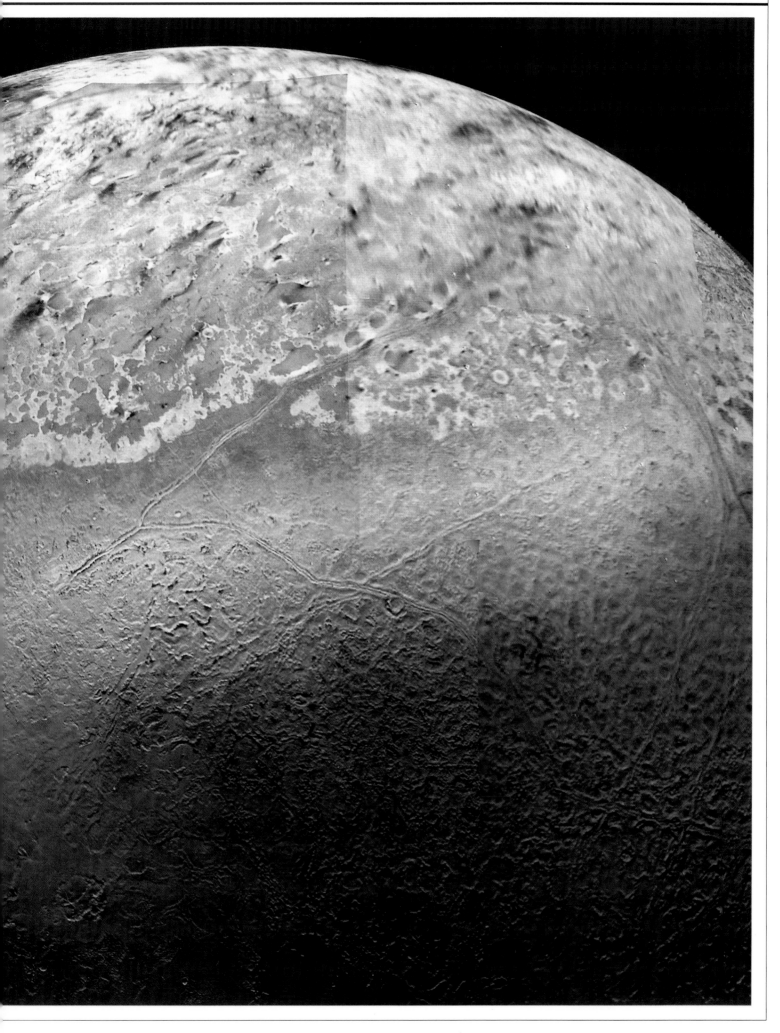

PLUTO

Above: These small sections of Clyde Tombaugh's 1930 discovery plates show images of Lowell's mathematically predicted trans-Neptunian planet, afterward named Pluto.

Prior to the observations undertaken in 1990 using the Hubble Space Telescope, the Solar System's outermost planet was also its most mysterious. Indeed, the very existence of Pluto was not confirmed until 1930! During the mid to late nineteenth century astronomers studying the revolutions of Uranus and Neptune detected slight anomalies that could be explained only by the gravitational effect of another body farther out in the Solar System. Around the turn of the century Percival Lowell (1855-1916) took up a systematic search of the heavens, looking for what he called 'Planet X.' When Lowell died in 1916, others continued the search, including William Pickering (1858-1938) of Harvard, who called the yet-undiscovered object 'Planet O.'

In 1915, and again in 1919, Pluto was actually *photographed but not noticed* because it was much fainter than it had been predicted to be. By this time, the organized search for Planet X was largely abandoned. In the meantime, Pickering altered his theory regarding the hypothetical location of Planet 'O,' and for the first time predicted that the perihelion of its orbit might actually bring it briefly closer to the Sun than Neptune. It was a radical idea that turned out to be accurate for Pluto.

In 1929 the Lowell Observatory at Flagstaff, Arizona, resumed the search begun by its founder, using a 13-inch telescope and a wide-field survey camera. This proved to be the right approach, and on 18 February 1930 the young astronomer Clyde Tombaugh (1906-) identified a new planet in some photographs he had taken the previous month. The discovery was announced a month later on the 149th anniversary of the discovery of Uranus, and the new planet was called Pluto after the Roman god of the dead and the ruler of the underworld. The name was considered appropriate because of the planet's enormous distance from the Sun's warmth, and also because the first two letters were Percival Lowell's initials.

In the first years after it was discovered, physical data about Pluto was virtually impossible to obtain. In 1950, however, Gerard Kuiper at the Mount Palomar Observatory estimated its diameter at 3658 miles, making it the second smallest planet in the Solar System. In 1965 it was observed in occultation with a 15th magnitude star, confirming that its diameter could not exceed 4200 miles. Thus it was that the 3658 estimate held until the 1970s. In 1976 methane ice was discovered to exist on Pluto's surface. Until then the planet's faintness had been attributed to its being composed of dark rock. Since ice would tend to reflect light more so than dark rock, it would follow that if it *were* 3658 miles in diameter *and* covered with methane ice, it would be brighter than it is. Therefore, it was decided that Pluto was smaller than originally suspected, leading us to conclude that its diameter is less than the 2160-mile diameter of the Earth's Moon, and probably as small as 1375 miles. This would make it the smallest of the nine planets and smaller than *seven* of the planetary moons.

It has also been suggested that Pluto is perhaps the largest of a theorized belt of trans-Neptunian asteroids. However, that notion fails to take into account that Pluto is two and a half times the diameter of Ceres, the largest known asteroid, and nearly seven times larger than the average of the 18 largest known asteroids. Among the arguments that *can* be made for its not being a planet, or at least for its not being a 'normal' planet, are the peculiar aspects of its behavior. As we have noted, it has an extremely elliptical orbit. This orbit ranges from an aphelion of 4.6 billion miles to a perihelion of 2.7 billion miles. The latter is actually closer to the Sun than the perihelion of Neptune's much more circular orbit, as Pickering had predicted. It has been pointed out that this highly elliptical orbit is more characteristic of asteroids, such as Hidalgo and Chiron.

A second aspect of Pluto's behavior that sets it apart from other planets is its steep inclination to the elliptic plane. The orbits of all the planets are within two-and-one-half degrees of this same plane, except Mercury, which is inclined at seven degrees, and Pluto itself, which is inclined at an acute 17 degrees, making it very unusual among its peers.

A theory concerning the physical nature of Pluto holds that at one time it was actually one of the moons of Neptune. It is further theorized that Pluto was somehow thrown out of its Neptunian orbit by some calamitous interaction with Neptune's moon Triton—perhaps even a collision. One of the Solar System's largest moons, Triton is more than twice the size of Pluto and, as such, might have had the gravitational force to slam a competing object out of Neptunian orbit if it ventured close enough. Both Triton and Nereid have unusual orbits that might possibly be relics of such a colossal event.

While its behavior partially defines it, and certainly sets it apart from other planets, less is known about Pluto's physi-

cal characteristics than is known about any other planet. Since no spacecraft will visit it in the twentieth century, we are left with only educated guesses about Pluto. We know that it is extremely cold, with noontime summer temperatures rarely creeping above −350 degrees Fahrenheit. Its rocky surface is known to also contain methane, probably in the form of ice or frost. Water ice may also be present, though this is not likely, and Pluto's mass suggests a rocky core. Pluto has generally been thought to have no atmosphere because its relatively small mass wouldn't give it sufficient gravity to retain an atmosphere, and it is too cold for even such a substance as methane to easily exist in its gaseous state. However, Scott Sawyer of the University of Texas has discovered what may be a tenuous methane vapor atmosphere on Pluto.

The discovery of the Plutonian moon Charon came about indirectly in 1978. While James Christy at the US Naval Observatory in Flagstaff, Arizona was attempting to measure Pluto's size, he thought he'd noticed that it was not spherical. Further observations led him to the conclusion that the elongation he had observed was due to the presence of a satellite very close to Pluto. Further calculations indicated that this newly discovered body was as close as 10,563 miles from Pluto.

Charon revolves around Pluto every 153 hours, exactly matching Pluto's period, meaning that the same hemisphere of Charon faces the same hemisphere of Pluto at all times. (From Earth, we can observe only one side of the Moon's surface, but the Earth rotates against the revolution of the Moon, so that the Moon is visible regularly from most of the regions of the Earth's surface.)

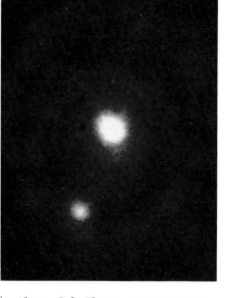

Above, left: **Pluto's enormous companion moon, Charon, was undetected, even by the best ground based telegraphs, until 1978.**
Above: **Launched in 1990, NASA's Hubble Space Telescope (HST) provides a much clearer image of the Solar System's most distant and enigmatic object, using the European Space Agency's Faint Object Camera. This image is the first long duration HST exposure ever taken of a moving target.**

In order to avoid smearing of the images, ground controllers had to pre-program the spacecraft to track Pluto accurately and compensate for the parallax introduced by the combined motions of Pluto, the Earth and HST in their respective orbits.

GLOSSARY

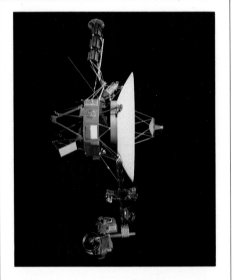

Above: Two identical 1800-pound Voyager spacecraft were launched by the United States on 20 August and 11 September 1977. Hopes were high for the two spacecraft which were destined for an unparalleled expedition into the distant reaches of the Solar System. Voyager 1 arrived at Jupiter on 5 March 1979 and proceeded on to Saturn. Passing the ringed planet on 15 August 1980, Voyager 1 was turned to fly past Saturn's moon Titan. From there, it continued toward the top of the Solar System which it exited during 1989.

Voyager 2, meanwhile, reached Jupiter on 10 July 1979, Saturn on 25 August 1981 and continued on toward Uranus. More than four years later, in January 1986, the tiny spacecraft finally reached Uranus and then set its sights on the edge of the Solar System.

On 25 August 1989, 12 years and five days after its launch, Voyager 2 reached Neptune, which was at the time, the outermost known planet in the Solar System. The brief glimpses of Uranus and Neptune revealed by Voyager 2 told us vastly more about those two planets than had been ascertained in human history or is likely to be learned in the lifetimes of those on hand for the 1986 and 1989 flybys.

Overleaf: Voyager 2 looks upon Saturn's vast and complex ring system at the moment of its closest approach on 25 August 1981. Artist Don Davis based this painting on a computer-assembled simulation of the spacecraft's journey through the Saturn System. The distant Sun is seen (upper left) at a range of one billion miles (1.6 billion kilometers).

Albedo: A measure of an object's reflecting power; the ratio of reflected light to incoming light in which complete reflection would give an albedo of 1.0.

Aphelion: The point in an object's orbital path when it is farthest from the Sun. The opposite of Perihelion.

Astronomical Unit (AU): A unit of measurement used to calculate intra-Solar System distances. One AU is equal to the distance from the Earth to the Sun, or 93 million miles. The following are the mean distances from the Sun of the nine known planets:

planet	mean distance
Mercury	0.387 AU
Venus	0.723 AU
Earth	1.000 AU
Mars	1.524 AU
Jupiter	5.203 AU
Saturn	9.539 AU
Uranus	19.182 AU
Neptune	30.058 AU
Pluto	39.439 AU

Conjunction: The alignment of two celestial bodies as viewed from a fixed point, such as from the Earth.

Eccentricity: Eccentricity describes how elongated is an elliptic orbit. Eccentricity equals the distance between the foci divided by the major axis (which is twice the mean distance). An eccentricity of zero is a circle. For the planets, the mean distances and eccentricities are:

planet	mean distance	eccentricity
Mercury	0.387 AU	0.206
Venus	0.723 AU	0.007
Earth	1.000 AU	0.017
Mars	1.524 AU	0.093
Jupiter	5.203 AU	0.048
Saturn	9.539 AU	0.056
Uranus	19.182 AU	0.047
Neptune	30.058 AU	0.009
Pluto	39.439 AU	0.250

Ecliptic: The plane in which the Earth revolves around the Sun. All the planets except for Pluto (17 degrees) and Mercury (7 degrees) revolve around the Sun in planes that are within 3.4 degrees of ecliptic, which is zero degrees.

Ellipse: A geometrical shape such that the sum of the distances from any point on it to two fixed points (called the foci) is constant. All the planets have more or less elliptical orbits; a circle is a type of ellipse, but an *elliptical orbit* describes a planetary path that is more eccentric than concentric.

Elliptical orbit: An orbit that is not *concentric*, or circular, but shaped like an *eccentric* ellipse. All of the planets, except Pluto, have orbits that are very nearly perfectly circular. Pluto has an 'elliptical orbit.' Comets have *very* elliptical orbits.

Light Year: A unit of measurement that equals the distance that light travels in one year at a speed of 186,281.7 miles per second.

Magnetosphere: The theoretically spherical region surrounding a star or planet that is permeated by the magnetic field of that body.

Magnitude: The brightness of a star or other celestial body as viewed from Earth with the naked eye on a clear night. The scale ranges from Magnitude 1, the brightest, to Magnitude 6, the faintest.

Mare: A 'sea' as observed on Earth's Moon. It is actually a vast, open basalt plateau and not a 'sea' in the sense of the Earth's seas. The plural is 'maria.'

Perihelion: The point in an object's orbital path when it is closest to the Sun. The opposite of Aphelion.

Protostellar: 'Pre-Star' (adjective). A term used in reference to the materials (hydrogen and helium) that *will become* a star, while they are still a 'pre-star' gas cloud.

Sidereal Period: For objects in the Solar System, the duration of time taken for a body to make a complete orbit, or revolution, around the Sun. This translates as that body's year. The Earth's sidereal period is 365.256 days. In a broader sense, a sidereal period is the orbital, or rotational, period of any object with respect to the fixed stars, or as seen by a distant observer.

Synodic Period: The orbital, or rotational, period of any object as seen by an observer on the Earth. For the Moon or a planet, the synodic period is the interval between the repetitions of the same phase or configuration.

INDEX

Allegheny Observatory 54
Amalthea 44, 45, *46*
Amata crater (Saturn) *6*
Antoniadi, Eugenios 35
Aphrodite Terra (Venus) 11, 23
Apollo 28, 2, *2*, 30, *31*
Appalachians 26
A Ring 54, 60
Arsia Mons (Mars) 34
Ascraeus (Mars) 34
Asteroid 6, 9, 11, 38, 39, 77
Asteroid belt 6, *6*
Atalanta Plain (Venus) 21
Atlantic Ocean 23
Atlantis (Space Shuttle Orbiter) 21
Aurora Borealis 14

Beta Regio (Venus) 21
Bode, Johann Elert 39
Bond, GP 59
B Ring 54

Callisto *42, 44,* 50, 51, 60, 61
Caloris Basin (Mercury) 16
Carrington, Richard 14
Cassini, Giovanni Domenico 18, 34, 54, 58, 59, *60*
Cassini Division 54
Celestial Police 39
Challenger Deep 24
Charon (Pluto's moon) 28, 77, *77*
Christy, James 77
Chryse Planitia (Mars) 36
Comets 6, 9, *11*
Continental drift 24
Copernicus Crater (Moon) 31

D'Arrest, Heinrich Ludwig 66
Davis, Don 80
Deimos (moon of Mars) 37, 38
Delta ring 64
Diana Chasma (Venus) 21, 26
Dione *2-3, 54-56, 61*

Earth 4-5, 6, 8, 9, 14, 16, 19, 21 23-28, 30-32, 34, 40, 42, 45, 46, 50, *51,* 54, 59, 61, 62, 68, 72, 77
Encke, Johann Franz 54
Encke Division 63
Epsilon Ring 63, 64
Europa (asteroid) 39

Europa (moon of Jupiter) *42, 44,* 45, 50, *50*

F Ring 54, 60

Galileans 44, *44,* 45, 61
Galilei, Galileo 14, 30, 44, 45, 54, 66
Galileo regio 50
Galle, Johann 66
Ganymede (moon of Jupiter) *40, 44,* 45, 50, 51, *51,* 60, 61
Goddard Space Flight Center *15*
Great Dark Spot 67, 68, *69*
Great Red Spot (Jupiter) 42, *42,* 54, *67,* 68
Greenhouse effect 18, 26
G ring 60

Hall, Asaph 38
Hall crater (Mars) 38
Halley's comet *11*
Hawaii 26
Heliopause 9, 15
Hellas Basin (Mars) 26
Hencke, Karl Ludwig 39
Herschel, William *30,* 34, 59, *60,* 62, 65
Himalayas 24
Hooke, Robert 42
Hubble Space Telescope 76, 77
Huygens, Christiaan 34, 54, 59, 60

International Astronomical Union 39
Io (moon of Jupiter) 26, *42, 44, 46, 48,* 50,
Ishtar Terra (Venus) 21, 23
Ithaca Chasma *61*

Jupiter 8, 9, 11, 16, 39, 40-52, *40-44, 46,* 61-63, 66, 68, 72, *78*

Keeler, James 54
Keeler gap 54
Kilauea 26
Kowal, Charles 46
Kuiper, Gerard 71, 72, 76

Lagrangian satellites 58, 60
Lakshmi Planvin (Venus) 21, *23*

Lassell, William 59, 65, 71, 72
Lesser Dark Spot *66,* 68
Lick Observatory 46
Lowell, Percival 16, 35, 50, 76, *76*
Luna 3 (Soviet) 30

Magellan 18, 21, *23*
Mare Fecunditatius 30
Mare Imbrium 30
Mare Orientale 30
Mare Tranquilium 30
Marianas Trench 24
Mariner spacecraft (United States) 16, *16, 17,* 18, 20, 35
Mariner's Valley (Mars) 34
Mars 6, 8, 9, *11,* 16, 24, 26, 31-39, *32-38,* 50, 59, 61
Mauna Kea 26
Mauna Loa 26, 34, *36*
Maxwell Mountains (Venus) 21, *23,* 24
Mercury 6, 8, 9, 11, 16, *16, 17,* 18, 26, 30, 60, 77
Meteorites 6, *6,* 11, 30, 38
Meteoroids 6
Meteors 6
Mimas *2-3, 55, 56, 60*
Moon 11, 16-18, 26, 28, *28, 30, 31,* 32, 38, 45, 76
Mount Everest 21, 24, 34
Mount Olympus (Mars) 24, 32, 34
Mount St Helens 26, 48

Neptune *1,* 7, 9, 52, 62, *66,* 68, *68-75,* 70-72, 76, 77
Nereid 70, 72, *72,* 77
Nicholson, SE 46

Olbers, Heinrich 39

Pacific Ocean 24, 26
Pavonis Mons (Mars) 34
Pele (Io) 48, 50
Perrine, CD 46
Phobos (moon of Mars) 36, 38, *38*
Photosphere 14
Piazzi, Guiseppe 39
Pickering, William 59, 76, 77
Pioneer 19, 20, 21, 23, 54
Pluto 7, 9, 28, 60, 76, 77, 77
Plutonian moons 77

Rhea (moon of Saturn) *2-3,*

55, 56, 60
Rhea Mons (Venus) 21
Roche crater (Mars) 38
Rocky Mountains 26

Saturn *2, 3,* 8, 9, 16, 42, 46, 52- 61, *54-56,* 62, 63, 66, 68, 78
Schiaparelli, Giovanni 16, 35
Schroeter, Johann Hieronymous 16, 18, 39
Shepard, Alan *31*
Skylab *12*
Solar flares *12,*
South Tropical Disturbance 42
Soviet Union 20, 30
Stickney crater (Mars) 38
Sun *4-5,* 6, 9, *10,* 11, *11,* 12, *13,* 14, 16, 18, 26, 28, 30, 34, 40, 42, 62, 66, 76, 77, *80*
Sunspots 14, *14*
Supernova 9
Syrtis Major (Mars)
Tharsis Region (Mars) *33,* 34

Theia Mons (Venus) 21
Tibetan plateau 24
Titan (moon of Saturn) 11, 54, 60, *61,* 70, *78,*
Titius of Wittenburg 39
Tombaugh, Clyde 76, *76*
Triton (moon of Neptune) 26, 46, 66, *66,* 70, 71, 72 *72, 74, 75,* 77
Tycho crater (Moon) 31

Uranus 8, 9, 52, 62-66, *63, 64,* 68, 70, *70,* 76, 78
Utopia Planitia (Mars) 36

Venera 20, 23
Venus *4-5,* 6, 8, 9, 16, 18, *19-21,* 24, 26, 34, 38, 59, 61
Viking spacecraft *32,* 35, *35, 36,* 37, *38*
Volcanos *21, 23, 33, 35,* 72
Voyager *1, 4-5, 10,* 42, 44, 45, 46, *47,* 48, *48,* 52, *54,* 56, 57, 58, 59, 62-66, *62, 63, 66,* 68, *68,* 70, 71, 72, *72-75, 78, 80*

Y Feature (Venus) 23